Ridiculous Adventures in Suburbia: Best of the West Virginia Surf Report

Volume One

Jeff Kay

Printed in the United States of America

ISBN 978-0-9833358-1-8

Book design: Polgarus Studio
Cover design: Iram Shahzadi

Smoking Fish Media
P.O. Box 313
Chinchilla, PA 18410
www.SmokingFishMedia.com

Contents

Introduction

When I was eight years old one of my girl cousins from Ohio allowed me to have a look at the copy of MAD magazine she'd been reading, and some kind of switch was flipped inside me. And it's never really been unflipped. It was so rude and antisocial, and not at all like the Archie comics I'd been reading. It felt so right.

That was a long time ago, and I can still remember where I was sitting, the general weather conditions, and the other people in the room. It's not an exaggeration to say it was one of the key moments of my early life. I became fully obsessed with MAD, and later The National Lampoon. This fact seemed to concern my parents and other adults around me, which only made it that much more exciting.

I wanted to be a comedy writer, I decided, and eventually began sending out packets of jokes to people like Johnny Carson and Phyllis Diller. I received a handwritten note of encouragement from one of the founders of the Lampoon, which was enough to keep me going. But, nobody wanted to buy any of my "hilarious" offerings.

So, I just started publishing them myself. During the mid-1980s I launched a homemade magazine, which I dubbed The West Virginia Surf Report. My home state is land-locked, you see… Good stuff.

That zine continued, off and on, until the late '90s, when I started reading an online journal by a woman named Krista Garcia. This was years before the word existed, but it was what would eventually be called a blog. Krista had published a zine herself, but I liked her online stuff even more. She'd recently moved from Oregon (I think) to New York City, and just wrote about her daily adventures there. It was hilarious, relatable, and fantastic.

And so… I copied Krista Garcia and launched my version of what she was doing in late 2000. For branding purposes I carried over the name of my zine, and began writing about my day-to-day life, trying to make it as funny and entertaining as possible. We'd recently moved from Southern California to Northeastern Pennsylvania, so there was a lot of culture shock to talk about. Plus, I'd just started a new job, which is always a good time.

The website continues to this day. It looks a lot different, but it's somehow survived. About a year ago I started thinking about maybe publishing edited versions of the early archives as ebooks and paperbacks. I thought there were enough funny stories and ideas to sustain such a thing. And I'm finally getting around to doing it. What follows is a collection of Surf Report posts from October 2000, when the site was launched, through the end of 2001.

A few quick notes about this little exercise:

This isn't just a copy and paste of the archives. I went through and edited out a lot of stuff. Believe me, this is a positive. I attempted to keep the things that made me smile, and enough of the random and ragged stuff to maintain the general feel of the site. This is a "best of," based on my reactions during the first read-through of this material in many years.

There's a lot of funny stuff, I was relieved to see. But some of it feels a bit self-conscious, like I didn't trust my abilities. However, there were also plenty of moments that made me think, "Wow. That's pretty clever. Wonder if I'd be able to come up with that line today? Probably not." And so, in classic fashion, I figured out a way to dump on myself across a considerable expanse of time.

There's probably too much profanity. I took some of it out, but left a lot.

This goes back to the self-consciousness, and the thinking that I could spice things up with a handful of curse words. I got better with time, but the first couple of years are foul-mouthed indeed.

Toney and I had two young kids during this first year, but I didn't mention them at the website. I made that decision because they were innocent and trusting, and it just didn't feel proper to me. I didn't want to write about my sweet, smiling boys alongside a story about my friend Kevin receiving a handjob at work. Ya know? Eventually I was outed, possibly during Year Two, and had to come clean. But our kids are not mentioned once here. You'll notice, however, that I was watching a lot of Spongebob. That probably should've tipped some people off.

There are some politically incorrect phrases and concepts in this book. But it was written in 2000-2001, basically for the benefit of my high school buddies. Also, there's a lot of "boy humor," as they say. But, what are you going to do? I grew up on MAD and The National Lampoon. And I'm a, you know, boy.

Near the end of this thing I talk a lot about a Mike Piazza paycheck that I got my hands on, and posted at the site. It was a scan of one of his actual bi-weekly payroll checks from the New York Mets, in the amount of $533,239.45. A friend sent it to me, I shared it with the readers, and all hell broke loose. I'm not sure this was explained very well, so I thought I'd do it now.

There's a lot of beer talk (a lot!), my super-strong opinions about consultants was surprising (chill, dude), and we certainly stayed busy back then (crazy!).

I'm as happy as I'll allow myself to be with these updates. They're rough, and occasionally cringe-inducing. But I think I did a decent job of zeroing-in on the absurdity of everyday life. I believe that's why the website became so popular. If I do one thing well, that's probably it.

I hope you enjoy this first volume. I plan to do others, possibly one for every year before the big move to Wordpress in 2008. Let me know your thoughts. And thanks for reading!

Jeff Kay

www.TheWVSR.com
www.SurfReportArchives.com

October 16, 2000

I think I'm going to enjoy this. One of the main reasons I was attracted to writing in the first place was because it allows a person the opportunity to pursue a creative project, while being hidden far away from the rest of the world. Generally speaking, I'm attracted to activities that are normally done in solitary, if not in secret. <insert own joke here>

It never occurred to me to dream of being a rock star, or a comedian, or an actor, or anything like that. That would be like wishing for a goiter, or a lazy eye; it would only draw attention. And that's the last thing I wanted.

And that's how it's always been. After I realized I probably couldn't swing the cost for the equipment needed to launch a 50,000-watt pirate radio station from my bedroom (a childhood dream), I considered writing as an alternative.

It too could be done behind closed doors, for considerably less money. And so, I began to fantasize of an underground bunker, or Unibomber shed out in the woods, with all the necessary tools to create brilliance. That, I knew, was the only thing that held me back. Privacy, and the right equipment. If I ever got those things — watch out! Now, twenty years later, almost everything's in place.

This site is done literally underground, in a tiny room in the corner of my basement. I've got a bad-ass computer, and a load of cool software. I've got a stereo, and a bookshelf full of reference material. I've even got a little refrigerator in the corner to cool my bottles of St. Louis writing elixir. Yes, I finally have my creativity bunker, and it's equipped with all the right tools. It's time to get down to business.

I even realized the other day, with some satisfaction, that websites like this could be considered modern-day pirate radio. But it's not the only thing I've got cooking. Not by a long-shot. I'm also preparing to exorcise the novels, and all those crazy screenplays that have been percolating in my brain for the last couple of decades. These are earth-shattering developments, my friends. The future is upon us.

And I'm gonna start the ball rolling as soon as I get a laser printer. I need a laser printer before I can really get serious. That's the final piece of the puzzle. But I'll be ready soon. Very soon. You should prepare yourselves now. I'm about to blow up. As soon as I buy just one or two more items.

October 17, 2000

I hate to smell men.

There's a kid in the office where I work who reminds me of this fact almost every day. He's young, barely out of his teens, and is obviously still struggling with some personal odor awareness issues. I picture him sitting in a galvanized washtub with a turkey baster full of cologne, marinating himself every morning before leaving the house. It's grotesque. Some people argue that at least he doesn't stink. I say it depends on your definition. BO, of course, shouldn't happen in the year 2000 — we have the technology — but I think the other end of the spectrum should be avoided as well. Either way, when he passes my desk, I smell a man. And it makes my stomach churn.

Perfume, pit-funk, mustiness, dirty clothes, grease, mustard, an aura of Frito-Lay products, etc. all fall into the same category , as far as I'm concerned. Men should smell like nothing. It's a noble pursuit that every male should embrace. I'm not really joking here. It's an important issue. I may contact Esquire about it.

October 24, 2000

Friday night my wife Toney and I drove to Philadelphia to see The Beautiful South. Not too many years ago we went to shows regularly, but neither of us is too interested in that kind of thing anymore. I fought it off as long as I could, but I finally had to admit that it was no longer fun. The thought of standing in a crowded smoky firetrap in the middle of the night in a urine-scented neighborhood full of freaks and predators, and laying down large sums of money for a few cans of get-drunk beer, has somehow lost its allure during my advancing years. It'll probably seem pathetic to some of you, but I've become extremely selective in who I'm willing to leave the house for. And Toney simply won't go "unless The Clash get back together or The Beautiful South play…or Kurt Cobain rises from the grave." I could come up with a dozen or so others, but there aren't many. The list has shortened drastically over the years, believe me.

The South Street area of Philly is really cool. It's one of those "bohemian" areas you can find in most big cities. But this one is unusually large, and impressively vibrant. Both sides of the narrow one-way street were lined with cars, leaving only a car-wide slot through which to navigate, and the sidewalks were absolutely teeming with people. The doors to the hipster shops, bars, record stores and trendy eateries were flung open and folks were wandering from business to business covered in the full gamut of fashions. The Parade of Nations at the opening ceremonies of the Olympics came to mind. It was an assault on the senses, and I was digging it, but where the hell was I gonna park in this mad house? It was getting late, my ass was knotting up from the 130-mile drive, and it didn't seem like there was much of a chance of finding a parking space within a five mile radius of this mess. And who knew what atrocities awaited us if we ventured down one of the side streets? My old Atlanta fear of being gutted and my skin turned into a junkie's smoking jacket stirred inside me. Oh, and I worried about my wife's welfare too.

After I asked one of the 10,000 or so cops where I could land my Toyota, we found ourselves in front of a parking garage around a corner from the main drag. A large man who resembled Seal suddenly appeared in the windshield, his face drawn back in a frightening rictus, waving maniacally for me to pull into the garage. So I buckled under the pressure and did as I was told. Once inside there were not only no parking spaces, but cars were actually parked in front of the exits. And even though the building obviously had several levels, cars were parked in front of all the ramps as well. What the hell? Whenever we turned a corner we found ourselves in a dark dead-end, which we'd have to back out of. It was nuts. And as we were driving around backwards, like fools, more and more cars continued to pour into the place as Seal literally scared up business outside. I thought Allen Funt was going to jump out from behind one of the pillars and give us a big hug. Finally we were able to escape through the same hole we entered, at a high rate of speed — both of us saying "holy shit" and "goddamn" a lot.

We found a regular open-air parking lot down the block and noted that the fee was a very reasonable four bucks. Cool! Problem solved.

The band was incredible. This was the third time we had seen them, and they always put on a great show. Main-man Paul Heaton moves around the stage like a person caught up in a swarm of bees, and he has a distinctive, smooth voice that never fails to amaze. Plus, the band always seems to be having as much fun as the audience, which is mightily infectious. They did a nice mix of older tunes and a bunch off their new album, Painting It Red, which comes out 10/31. What always strikes me about these guys is the fact that they don't get airplay, and sometimes don't even have an American record label, but their shows are always sold out and the audience knows every word to every song. I alternate between being glad they're not as hugely popular in the US as they are everywhere else, and disgusted that stupid Americans overlook them. But it's cool to be able to see them in a small venue like the Theater of the Living Arts. You feel like you're getting away with something.

As we were preparing to end our pleasant evening out in the big city I thought I understood the parking lot guy to be saying, "fifteen dollars" but knew logically I must be mistaken. "What was that?" I said. "Fifteen dollars," he repeated. When I started to protest he just calmly held up his hand (he'd been through this bullshit before) and said, "Bottumadasign, bottumadasign." At the bottom of the sign there was a tiny asterisked note that said something along the lines of '$15.00 Flat Rate on Weekends.'

And we made our way home. This time it was only me saying "holy shit" and "goddamn" a lot, as well as "fifteen dollars!!" Toney seemed unusually calm.

October 30, 2000

I saw a commercial a few days ago that momentarily froze my brain in confusion. I knew the TV wasn't tuned to Comedy Central, but my inner sensors instantly told me the ad couldn't be anything but a joke. It was for McDonald's, and was trumpeting their "McToberfest" promotion, and — get this - their new bratwurst sandwiches! For a brief second I thought a Saturday Night Live parody had been injected into the middle of CNN Headline News for some unknown reason. Hence, my mini-meltdown.

Of course, it wasn't a joke. McDonald's, at least the northeastern Pennsylvania locations, is serving up bratwurst! Can you imagine anything more disgusting? What's next, shellfish? Moo Goo Gai Pan? Duck?

I had to have one.

Truthfully, I've always been slightly suspicious of any meats sold in "links". Maybe it's the casing, which is undoubtedly made from intestines, and sometimes snaps when you bite it. Or it could be the mysterious mixture of stuff that comprises the guts of the things. Who knows if it's real meat or just ground up scrotums and buttholes? For some reason I've always been mildly wary that I'd find a human toenail in one someday. I can handle hotdogs, because they're familiar, but any of their cousins in the link family creep me out. I remember going to Cincinnati as a kid and seeing big frightening white sausages of some sort rotating slowly on those stainless steel hotdog machines all over town. I had a hard time even looking at them. And years later when I got up enough nerve to actually eat a kielbasa, I remember the hunks of it seemed to actually grow in my mouth as I chewed. Horrifying! But they taste pretty damn good. That, I must admit.

Disgusting or not, I love the idea of trying out test-marketed foods, that are usually ill-conceived if not completely crackpot in nature. No doubt they'll be gone forever in a month's time, and nobody will believe they ever existed in the future. Like green ketchup, for instance. So today I went to McDonald's, before the month ended, and celebrated McToberfest in style. I opted for the meal-deal, which gets you a bratwurst sandwich, medium fries, and a medium drink for $2.99.

Maybe it was my imagination but there seemed to be a strange smell wafting from the kitchen that I'd never noticed before. I was careful to notice if the cashier would give me an "are you sure about that?" look, but she didn't even flinch when I placed my order. And the workers in the back didn't peer around the corner to see who was foolish enough to actually buy one of those things, or anything like that. It was almost as if people purchased bratwurst at McDonald's all the time. It was no big deal. Amazing.

It looked like a turd, and it was a little larger than I had anticipated. It was on a hotdog bun, and came with mustard and (red) ketchup. And unfortunately, for storytelling's sake, it didn't taste too terrible. In fact, it tasted a lot like their hamburgers. Of course, everything at McDonald's tastes pretty much the same, and their big fat sausage sandwich falls right into line. I have little doubt that it is completely indigestible, and will be lodged in the walls of my gut the day they finally crate me up. But it's been several hours since I ingested it and my bowels don't feel any more stormy than normal. Too bad. I was kind of hoping I'd get back to work and explode in a fountain of diarrhea, sending my co-workers shrieking for the exits. But it didn't happen. Maybe it'll have the opposite, less dramatic, effect. If so, I'll tell you all about it.

Stay tuned…

November 8, 2000

— A few weeks ago a teenage girl was murdered in the Wendy's that I frequent, close to where I work. It's a horrible story. She was an 18 year old assistant manager, and was supposed to start college the very next day. When she was preparing to open the place early on a Sunday morning, somebody killed her and reportedly mutilated her body in the kitchen of the restaurant. A couple of days later police arrested a maintenance man who worked there, and charged him with the murder. It was a terrible, tragic occurrence and received wall-to-wall coverage on all the local news channels for days. The restaurant stayed closed for about a week, while authorities completed their investigations, but then it finally re-opened — to mild protest. Many felt that the place should be torn down, or at least radically remodeled. I heard lots of folks vow that they'd never set foot in there again, because the "vibes" would be too creepy. Indeed, the few times I was there right after it reopened I pretty much had the run of the joint. I assumed it wouldn't stay in business long, but today it was packed, just like it used to be. I guess juicy burgers and tasty chicken sandwiches triumph over bad vibes in the long run.

— And finally, some election day totals:

The Drudge Report 2,753,186 pageviews

TheWVSR.com 184 pageviews

That means that on the average, Matt Drudge and I received 1.3 million visitors to our sites yesterday. Thanks America!

November 16, 2000

For some reason I'm in a biography phase. I read as much as I can, and most of the time I read fiction. But a couple of weeks ago I finished a really good book about Raymond Chandler, and now I'm into Let It Blurt, a

Lester Bangs bio. Behind that is Stephen King's On Writing and Mr. Mike: The Life and Work of Michael O'Donoghue. I can't explain the sudden obsession with other people's lives and, truthfully, it probably wouldn't benefit anyone if I tried to figure it out. I'll save that for my next visit to John K's Pub (tomorrow).

But a few brief thoughts about Raymond Chandler, if I might:

After spending his early days being educated in Europe, serving in WW1, and bumming around the US, he finally settled in southern California. There he found a job with an oil company, as an accountant. Over the next dozen or so years he was a man possessed, pouring himself into his job completely. He climbed the corporate ladder and eventually became a high-paid executive. But then he got bored. And he started to drink - heavily. After he began showing up at work blasted, or not at all, the company had no choice but to fire him. And that's where the legend began.

He went through the painful process of getting himself off booze, and made the decision to live off his savings while he taught himself to be a novelist. He used the same obsessive determination that fueled his early oil days, to learn the craft of writing. He re-wrote famous scenes in literature, and figured out the techniques the original authors used to make them so much better. He horizontally cut his typing paper into thirds, and made a vow that there would be a little "magic" on each sheet when he wrote. He worked at it all day, every day. Soon he was submitting detective stories to the pulp magazines of the day, and made something like $750 the first year he was a professional writer.

Of course, he went on to invent one of the most famous literary characters in history, Philip Marlowe, and became an international celebrity and millionaire. And he didn't publish his first novel until age 50.

This is, of course, a very inspiring story to people like myself who cling to some pathetic little thread of hope that it could still happen, even though the clock is ticking. Of course, I know deep-down I probably don't have the focus and discipline required for even Chandler's drunken years. When you read biographies of great people, you start to see a pattern: they're all almost maniacally driven. Chandler pushed everything to its limits, even his drinking problem. That's not really me, and it's not really 99.999% of people. I'm convinced there are folks all around us who are as clever and bright as Raymond Chandler, or Stephen King, but since they don't possess the fire in their belly to develop it, they'll never be recognized. It's sad, but true.

But don't count me out completely. I'm going to start kicking ass — right after Thanksgiving.

November 25, 2000

Toney and I went to my parents' house in West Virginia for the Thanksgiving holiday, and spent much of Thursday kicking ourselves for not having the foresight to sneak in a flask of hard liquor. Thursday was simply excruciating. Of all the things I'm thankful for, the fact that Thanksgiving is now over ranks high on the list.

My parents, and pretty much my entire extended family, don't drink. I never understood such destructive behavior, and have had the personal strength to break that crazy cycle in my own life. It wasn't easy, but what important achievements are? And if ever there was a time that confirmed that booze is nearly a necessity in certain situations, it was this past Thursday in my parents' living room in suburbia surrounded by relatives, and more relatives.

All the cliches were there: loud elderly women invading people's space with their entire heads, screaming kids, irritating personalities, a blaring TV, pissed off people sulking in silence, dogs barking, people smacking their lips like livestock struggling with a caramel, and long extended periods of sheer dullness — all with nothing stronger than coffee to help see you through it.

I've spent holidays with Toney's family, as well as with various girlfriend's families, through the years, and know my own is no more irritating than most. But usually there's some uncle performing the public service of mixing strong drinks in the kitchen. Anything else is like natural childbirth, and what right-thinking person would willingly choose that?

After the throngs of people either left or wandered outdoors in an attempt to "walk off" dinner, Toney and I shot-gunned three each of the Bud Lights my Dad keeps in the back of the refrigerator for special occasions. I'm pushing forty and found myself frantically burying our empties in the trashcan beneath globs of discarded mashed potatoes, stuffing, and corn. How pathetic is that?

But it's all over now, and I've got a powerful bourbon and Coke sweating on the coaster beside my monitor as I type this — deep underground in the Surf Report bunker, with Muswell Hillbillies playing.

Hell yeah.

A BLAST FROM THE PAST: A few years ago I was in Reno, NV at my wife's mother's tiny apartment for Thanksgiving dinner. Again, there was a small army of people present. Right in the middle of the meal Toney's brother pushed away from the table and excused himself. He walked straight into the bathroom and let loose a high-pressure rectal explosion that was clearly audible at the dinner table. Everybody just looked at their plates and pretended they heard nothing. A few minutes later he returned, and said "Could somebody pass the rolls?" as if nothing had happened. Luckily, we were all appropriately drunk.

December 2, 2000

— I was in a restaurant a few days ago and the hostess looked me up and down and said, "Non-smoking, right?" It was one of the proudest moments of my life.

— I've never subscribed to the popular belief that people in various regions of the country are radically different from one another. I've lived all over, and people are basically the same wherever you go. In fact, I get a little irritated when I hear people stereotype the South, or California, or West Virginia, or most any other place. It's just ignorance, in most cases. But I must go on the record and say that I think northeastern Pennsylvania has an unusually high concentration of bad drivers. I spent years effortlessly navigating some of the worst traffic in the world, in Atlanta and Los Angeles, but the roadways here shred my nerves. Before I moved I don't think I've ever seen a person backing down an interstate entrance ramp, for instance. Now I see it about once a week. And any right-thinking person knows that the speed limit is only a suggestion, not something you're supposed to actually adhere to. But the worst offense, the one that will probably get me killed someday, is the mind-boggling tendency of people here to come to a complete stop — WHEN MERGING ONTO AN INTERSTATE! These fools drive to the end of the entrance lane, with their blinker on, and STOP to wait for a break in the traffic! You don't do that! This is one of the basics! That lane is designed for acceleration, so you can join the flow of traffic at the going rate. I've barely averted slamming into the back of a half-dozen cars because of this, and I've never encountered it anywhere else. One of these days I'm going to be preoccupied with skipping a song on a Smithereens CD or something, not paying attention, and end up on the roof of a hardware store with a steering wheel in my hand covered in gasoline and fire.

— My workplace is currently crawling with consultants. Apparently it's time for The Company to drop a few million on some computer "upgrades", so out come the consultants. And if there's a group of people easier to hate, I'm not aware of it. Smug, arrogant, self-assured, young, well-dressed, highly-paid, educated bastards and bastardettes, one and all. God, how I hate them. But there's one from Raleigh, NC with a thick Southern accent, and for some reason he's a lot easier to take than the rest. I'm pretty sure it's the accent that makes the difference. It gives his air of absolute, soul-crushing superiority a sort of homespun appeal, that ultimately elevates him above the pack.

— My mother-in-law recently asked me if I've seen The Green Mile. I told her no, and that was her cue to tell me all about it. In a nutshell, she said it was a good movie but way too graphic. I assumed she meant it was too violent, but I should've known better. She went on to explain that it's "basically three hours of pissing." Those were her exact words. I started thinking about this and was a little surprised that an accomplished actor like Tom Hanks would take on a project based on pissing. Maybe a cameo in a small pissing picture by a director he admired, but a starring role? Warner should've used her quote on the video box: "Unquestionably the best picture of the year" -CBS-TV, "Explosive!" -Gene Shalit, "Basically three hours of pissing!" -Jeff's mother-in-law.

December 15, 2000

Earlier this week I woke up at around 1AM and felt like I needed to either puke or unleash a Wyoming-sized fart. I stumbled downstairs, groaning and clutching my stomach, and just as I lifted the lid on the toilet the suspense ended. Five or six powerful jets of whatever happened to be in my gut at the time came up — with authority. And I also shit my pants. About five times. Every time I heaved, a little something extra snuck out the rear exit as well. I was a walking lawn sprinkler of grossness. And then, as if that wasn't enough, the toilet overflowed. I kid you not. I don't know what happened there. I wasn't upchucking solid balls of anything. But over the top it all came, and into the floor. Yes, it was one of my prouder moments.

One minute I was sleeping peacefully in my warm bed, and the next I was mopping the bathroom in the middle of the night, sporting a beard of puke and a sizable load in my pants — my wife looking on in utter disgust. It was like an episode of The Lucy Show as written by Michael O'Donoghue.

December 29, 2000

— An actual quote from the Classmates.com message board for my old high school: *"Would this be the same Gene who won a dollar from Persinger by playing the b flat concert scale the fastest? One crazy sax, man! Your legacy lives on…"* Nerds.

— It's lung-bitingly cold here in northeastern PA, and I heard yesterday that we're going to get hit with a "snow bomb" this weekend. I don't know what that means, but don't like the sound of it. My instincts are telling me to buy large quantities of beer, which I fully intend to heed. I've learned that a man should trust his gut in situations like this, and the size of my gut is proof that I nearly always do. Please pray for me.

January 4, 2001

Well, it's 2001 and I have to say I'm pretty disappointed so far. I went back to work yesterday, and didn't see a single flying car. All I saw were the boring old fashioned kind that roll along the ground…on wheels! What a ripoff. I've been looking forward to this since I was nine years old. When I was a kid, the future was always represented by the year 2001 — and there were always flying cars. Where are the flying cars?! And where are the housecleaning robots named Rosie? And all the cool creatures walking around in people clothes, but with horse heads? Ripoff, a major ripoff. I haven't felt this disappointed since I met Hank Aaron.

Toney and I spent New Year's Eve cleaning the basement and, uh, drinking beer. It was quite a festive event. We have boxes that are still sealed from when we moved from Atlanta to Los Angeles in 1996. We're trying to weed out a bunch of the crap, so we don't have to keep transporting it and storing it. Toney's a lot better at it than I am. I simply cannot part with my endless cartons of old Creem magazines and classic issues of National Lampoon and Mad and Trouser Press (most with the flexi-disc still intact, thank you very much). And I'm not going to toss my albums, even though I don't have a turntable anymore, and I'll be damned if I'm giving up the contents of my childhood nightstand drawer. There are some important items in there, like cinnamon toothpicks and superballs and a five-pound transistor radio and Dum-Dum suckers from haircuts I got in 1976. It's hard to explain the importance of all this stuff to Toney, especially as she's building a massive trash pile out of old letters from dead relatives and school yearbooks and the like, but I did my damndest. She thinks I'm mentally ill.

But anyway, in one of the boxes I came across some old photos of me (taken by my girlfriend at the time), from around 1982 or 83. They're absolutely horrifying. I can't believe I went out of the house looking like that, and can't believe my parents or any of my friends didn't pull me aside for a little talk. In some I was wearing extremely tight shorts, the type that only gay men or Canadians would wear today. And I had a slight bubble-butt, and big-ass Gabe Kaplan hair. And the worst offense of all — the kind of pitiful wispy moustache that should be grounds for incarceration. I was a complete and absolute mess. Of course I was acting like an idiot in most of the shots as well, apparently to insure that the future humiliation would be absolute. The fact that Toney — my wife — spent about ten minutes buckled over in laughter with a photo of me in her hand says it all, I think. Sheesh.

January 7, 2001

— As I was flipping through the television channels the other day I noticed that American Movie Classics is showing Mel Brooks' Silent Movie. I saw that thing in the theater when it was first released, and now it's being presented on a nostalgia cable network like it's some rare old artifact from the days of yore. When that AMC museum curator guy strolls out and starts setting up a film with a reverence usually reserved for ancient paintings and pieces of Native American earthenware — and it's something that you remember seeing as a new release, it'll send chills up your spine. Damn. I've got to get me a mid-life crisis Camaro, and quick.

— Speaking of Viagra, have you seen that commercial they're running now with the good-looking guy in his forties apparently just happy as shit he's getting to go to the doctor that day to discuss his inability to achieve an erection? What's that all about? If I ever develop a hole in my inner tube, and everything goes flat on me, I certainly won't be skipping down the sidewalk, shaking hands and dancing about it. I'll probably resemble Mickey Rourke in Barfly. And why's the guy so young? Dear god, why's he so young? Should I go for a convertible, or just a T-top?

— The price of postage stamps go up today by one cent, so let the bitching begin. Whenever this happens, you can count on a bunch of blowhards to get up on their high horses, and pontificate in superior tones about the poor service and how unnecessary the rate increase is, blah blah blah. It's a penny. Shut up about it. If it were a dime increase, it would still be a great deal. The postal service does a damn good job, regardless of what it's popular to believe. Quit yer bitching, you bitter bastards. It's stamps.

— Yesterday I was sitting on the couch reading and Toney came home from the grocery store and spiked a gallon of milk in the middle of our living room floor. I couldn't believe my eyes. Milk was halfway up a wall, all over the floor, and covering us both from head to toe. She said she tripped over something, and dropped it, but I think she did it on purpose. Out of the corner of my eye I'm pretty sure I saw the jug raised above her head, right before the explosion. It will be interesting to see if this "tripping" becomes a pattern.

January 9, 2001

— I noticed a hole in one of my favorite t-shirts yesterday, and I'm preparing for the worst. It was purchased in a bar in Greensboro, NC called College Hill Sundries — one of my all-time favorite watering holes. I've literally had this shirt for a decade. It's gray and has the words College Hill Alumni on the front. It's served me through happy times and sad. I wore it at least once a week the whole time I was in Atlanta and L.A., during the many adventures I got myself into during those eventful years. And now it's starting to show its age. How do you calculate t-shirt years? I don't think they last as long as dogs, so maybe eight or nine for every people year? I don't know, but I know its days are numbered, and I'm not just being dramatic when I say I'm sad about it. You don't come across a perfect t-shirt every day. Please send cash donations in lieu of flowers.

— FYI - "Pouring lighter fluid on my genitals and setting them afire" appears just one spot below "Sitting down and watching an NBA game" on my checklist of Ideal Ways to Spend an Evening.

January 14, 2001

I received a call earlier this week from a guy I used to hang around with in Atlanta. He wanted to know if The Jenny Jones Show was filmed in Los Angeles or Chicago. I told him I had no idea, and that seemed to confuse him — since I'm the obvious person one turns to when such questions arise(?!?). But he quickly moved on to some completely unrelated subject, and so began another typical conversation with Kevin from Atlanta.

Kevin's a good guy, and we've both made a half-assed effort to stay in touch over the years, but he's not the most focused or mature person I know. Of course, anybody who knows me knows that I don't exactly set new standards in those departments myself. But Kevin makes me look like William F. Buckley. Conversations with him inevitably lead to a lengthy discussion about his latest sexual conquests, and this one was no different.

He's older than me, probably forty or so, and is the horniest person I know. He's never been married, but goes out with countless women and apparently has a sex life that would impress a professional basketball player. He also has a real talent for giving vivid accounts of his exploits, full of the most graphic details, without coming across as being overly crude or rude. And maybe I'm naive, but I believe all of his stories. I really don't think he's a bullshitter. I'm almost sure of it.

His latest news is that he did the next logical thing and took a second job at night in a porn shop. Hell, I joked, the employee discounts alone could save him thousands. He laughed, and then the flood walls came down. He started by telling me that during his first week there a woman came in and ended up blowing him in the alley behind the store. And she left no DNA, if you get my drift. How does something like that happen? This is the type of situation that I can't even imagine. I've worked retail, and can't remember even holding hands with any of the customers.

Apparently the nighttime clientele of this joint also has a tendency to go behind the counter and vigorously rub the cashier's crotch before exiting. I don't know if this is some kind of porno culture vote of confidence or what, but he says women are constantly yanking down his zipper and giving him a hand, right there behind the cash register. What the hell's that? I've had employers jerk me off, but never customers. I told him I'd hate to see the tip jar in that place.

I asked if they only sold magazines, or what, and he said they also sell lubes and dildos and inflatable dolls and butt plugs and on and on and on. And he said they have a bank of those curtained booths where people can view adult films in private. They sell travel-sized packets of hand lotion and individual condoms for people's use in the booths, which really disgusts me. Maybe I'm a prude, but I couldn't work in a place where a parade of men flog their logs all night, just a few feet away from where I'm standing. I'd rather flip burgers, and that's not a euphemism.

He went on to tell me about selling dildos to wealthy Buckhead housewives, and how some of them are shy about it and won't make eye contact, while others proclaim they want something that will "fill me up completely." By that time I was starting to feel a little dirty, just hearing all this stuff. It sounds exciting at first, but realistically I'd never allow some random person to handle my organ, and I'd just as soon dip my goods in an open sewer before I'd let some demented stranger service me in an alley. I know I may have to turn in my guy card for saying this, but the whole notion of going to almost any length to get your rocks off is pretty creepy to me. I started steering the conversation to its end.

But just before we said our goodbyes, almost as an afterthought, he dropped one more bomb. He said that a few weeks ago he had gone home with a husband and wife he met at the store. And he had sex with the woman as her husband stood there with an erection and a camera, snapping off photos. That was too much. I mean, what is this, the '70's? I asked him if he was aware the pictures would undoubtedly end up on the internet, and he said that wasn't going to happen. Apparently he trusts these people, which tells you a lot right there.

One of my wife's friends thinks Kevin's obsession with sex is a "disease." I don't know about that, but I don't think there's any doubt it's at least clouding his judgment at this point. He supposedly was reprimanded at work recently for having a screen saver on his computer that showed a hair brush handle repeatedly entering and exiting a vagina(??). And going home with strangers you meet late at night in an Atlanta porn shop is a good way to enhance your chances for an early death. The guy is literally laying everything on the line for sex. I don't think I've ever been that horny.

At least not since high school.

January 22, 2001

— And so, I got to spend about two hours on Sunday morning shoveling the "little or no accumulation" out of our driveway, and it was a killer. I took a break at one point and told Toney that if she looked out the window and saw me laying in the yard, not to assume I'm making snow angels. Today I feel like I've been run over by a Jeep. My arms are jittery and buzzing, and I'm pretty sure the tip of my spine has snapped off at the base. I can feel shards of frayed bone grinding into the flesh of my upper-ass region as I walk. Even my love handles ache. If they don't start predicting more blizzards pretty soon, I'm going to end up in the hospital.

— Toney told me that she and her mother were walking through the K-Mart parking lot earlier this week, when an old red Honda pulled up beside them. A Korean man was driving, and he said, "Excuse me, are either of you ladies single?" They said no, and picked up their pace a little. He said, "My friend looking for an Asian lady or a white lady to marry. Are you sure you're not single?" They again said no, and then he sweetened the pot: "My friend very rich!" After they resisted even this final temptation, he moved on to another woman walking nearby. It may have taken him the better part of the day, but is there any doubt that this industrious young man is on his honeymoon right now?

January 29, 2001

In California we lived in a tiny house on a cul-de-sac absolutely crawling with kids. They were everywhere, and almost none were older than five. They scattered like chickens whenever a car entered the street, and they screeched and screamed from sun-up to sun-down. It sounds horrible, I know, but I actually enjoyed it in a way. That's pretty much how I grew up, running wild with other kids in the neighborhood, and I had thought that kind of thing wasn't possible anymore. So, for the most part, I got a kick out of it — in a nostalgic sort of way. But there were a couple of brothers among the flock who were a little troubling. They were WAY ahead of the other kids as far as motor skills and athletics were concerned. I used to joke that they probably skateboarded out of their mother's vagina. Predictably, they were also dumber than a box of rocks. Both were fairly mean and aggressive as well, and were almost free of supervision and parental guidance.

They exploded out their front door every morning before the dew was off the grass, and didn't call it a day until the sun went down. Their father worked constantly, and their mother almost never checked on them. Indeed, the younger of the two actually carried a hammer with him wherever he went, starting as soon as he was old enough to remain upright with it in his arms. This was a real full-sized carpenter's hammer, with a vicious-looking claw on one side. I was convinced somebody's head was going to get opened up like a can of Campbell's chowder during some tense dispute over stick-ownership or something, but luckily it never happened.

Other parents were constantly "discussing" the brother's latest antics with their Mom and Dad, to no avail. Unless you had proof, you see, you better tread lightly mister. And how dare you call into question their parenting skills! It's an old story, familiar to anyone who ever had the privilege of growing up. This went on for a long time, but things finally came to a head when the two started shitting in people's yards. Whenever the urge hit them, they'd simply unbuckle their pants and drop a glistening load wherever they stood.

In this neighborhood a hammer-brandishing two year old was one thing, but humans pooping on sidewalks was over the line. And so, after more "discussions" with the parents, the boys started shitting only in their own yard. This was the compromise. They'd throw down a Wiffle Ball bat in the middle of a game, sprint into their front yard, take a big dump in front of the picture window, then return to the batter's box. After a while, they apparently got a little self-conscious and started only using the back yard. It was something we all just learned to live with. The neighborhood gossip was that the same thing went on inside the house as well, that the toilet was but one of many options available for the act of defecation. After all, you don't want to stifle a child's expressionism, right?

I had almost blocked out this chapter of my life when Toney received a call a few days ago from our old next-door neighbor, the mother of a five-year old boy. She just called to catch up, and things eventually turned to the two criminals-in-the-making. Nothing's reportedly changed in the year we've been gone. The public crapping continues to this day, and I can't help but think their piles have gotten bigger with age. She then went on to tell a story straight out of a horror movie.

She said her kid was outside playing recently, and when she went out to check on him he was nowhere to be found. She started screaming his name, growing more and more frantic. Finally he answered her back — and it sounded like his voice was coming from the brothers' back yard! She ran to the fence and looked in, and almost passed out at what she saw. He was in the backyard with the brothers, running around without shoes — in a field of feces. He was laughing and frolicking in a landscape of human waste. She said there were piles everywhere, that she'd never even seen anything like it in a zoo. She snatched him out of the yard and took him home and spent the rest of the afternoon scrubbing him down with anti-bacterial soap.

February 4, 2001

— Today I actually missed California a little bit. Usually when I miss a place it's tied to food or drink in some way, and this was no different. Toney and I decided to go out for lunch, and we were both craving Mexican for some reason. As I mentioned in my previous entry, this place is absolutely lousy with white people, and it's mighty difficult to find good Mexican or Chinese food — both of which were available in abundance in southern California. We decided on a place called Don Pablo's Mexican Kitchen, which is presumably a chain restaurant. It looks cool on the inside, if a bit contrived. It's open and airy with Christmas lights strung from the ceiling, and colorful mismatched furniture: a little bit of Tijuana right here in Scranton (yeah, right). The food wasn't bad, but it was a long way from good. Kinda bland, in an Olive Garden sort of way. And I'm almost certain the tacos had garlic in them. What the hell's that all about?! It made me long for LA, and the incredible burritos and enchiladas that could be had at a million little Mom and Pop establishments all over the city. As they say, you don't miss your water 'til the well runs dry.

— To be fair, northeastern Pennsylvania has its own lineup of kickass regional specialties. Specifically, cheesesteaks and pizza and Yuengling lager. If (when) my company calls and informs me my family and I will soon be living in yet another city, these are the things I'll miss. I need to enjoy them while I can. Lord knows, I've already done my best to enjoy the lager as much as possible.

— Speaking of regional foods, I stop in a coffee shop/bakery on my way to work two or three days a week. It's very NYC, and they sell big loaves of marble rye and black & white cookies and have stacks of the Times and the Post and the Village Voice lying around. And unlike the Mexican place, it's authentic. The women who work the counter are even angry bitches. It's uncanny.

— One last food item, before moving on. McDonald's, and other fast food joints, should immediately institute a policy barring cashiers from working if they have big purple hickies on their necks. I won't go back to the Mickey D's close to my work until enough time has passed for one to fade from a cashier's neck that works there. She's overweight and sassy and wears pink frosted lipstick. Maybe I'm overly sensitive, but I don't want to imagine a woman of this sort making out right before I eat my lunch. It's nasty — and they're really shooting themselves in the foot by alienating a man of my size.

— It's supposed to snow another eight inches tonight. I'd stick my head in the oven, if it weren't electric.

February 11, 2001

— My mother-in-law: "The Black Crowes aren't rock 'n' roll, they just play that new wave shit."

— I hate to keep harping on this, but more and more evidence continues to pour in that I'm getting really old. The last few days my back has ached, and this morning I could barely walk when I got out of bed. Lightning bolts of pain flashed from the base of my spine whenever I attempted to stand up straight, and when I put weight on my right foot it felt like somebody was plunging a steak knife into my back. I was walking around the house grimacing and flailing my arms like Joe Cocker. It was a pathetic display. Indeed, whenever the act of putting on a pair of underwear becomes a job equal to say, building a small birdhouse, it can only be viewed as pathetic. And on top of that I received an e-mail the other day concerning my twentieth high school reunion. Twentieth! I can remember when my parents went to their twentieth, and I thought they were older than dirt. And if this weren't enough, I watched on old Paul Newman movie last night on DVD called Fort Apache, The Bronx. I knew little about it, but it looked pretty good. It turned out to be only OK, but the real disappointing part was when I learned when it was made. The movie looked really dated, the cars and hairstyles were big and ridiculous, and the inner-city slang made me guess it was from around 1974. But it came out in 1981 — the same year I graduated from high school! It looked like a period piece. How utterly depressing.

February 14, 2001

— When I was driving to work this morning I saw an old battered pickup truck with a bumper sticker that said, "I (heart) my goats."

— I read an article the other day on the internet that quoted some doctor as saying the average size of an American male's erect penis is roughly the length of a Nokia cell phone, without the antennae. I own a Nokia cell phone and I don't appreciate this at all. Every time I make a call now I feel like I'm slapping some guy's schlong to the side of my face. The silver lining: my airtime charges will undoubtedly plummet this month. But I'm not really a fan of the analogy. Why do I get the feeling this doctor is on the payroll of the Motorola Corporation?

February 21, 2001

— I was in a Target store over the weekend and I couldn't remember what sized jeans I wear, so I just grabbed the biggest ones they had and went into the changing room. On the wall inside was a sign that said something like, "Please do not remove undergarments when trying on clothes." Apparently they've had a problem with this in the past, since they went to all the trouble of printing up the signs, and that instantly brought up several questions in my mind. First of all, why would a man take off his underwear in a Target changing room? And how would they know if he did? How did they know to print up those signs? Did they find skidmarks in a pair of khakis? Or do they have those creepy two-way mirrors? Is there an article of clothing that would necessitate the removal of underwear to make an informed buying decision? Surely people don't try on underwear itself do they? Then I started thinking about a guy walking up to the girl at the changing rooms and holding up a three-pack of Hanes briefs and saying, "Does this count as one or three?" Then I imagined him coming out with the package ripped open and two pairs still left in it, and another old worn out pair with the elastic coming loose and a giant skidmark, and handing it all back to her and saying, "No, they just don't look right on me." I was smiling like an idiot when I came out of the little room, and I'm sure security kept an eye on me until I left. Also, I washed my new jeans in HOT water when I got home, since that store is apparently crawling with people rubbing their naked balls all over the merchandise.

— When the hell does baseball season start? It seems like it's been a year since the World Series. Baseball is the only sport that matters. All the rest…don't matter.

February 26, 2001

I bit the bullet and went shopping for clothes over the weekend. This is something I almost never do. I know most people buy clothes continuously, and it's a never-ending mission by design. Not me. It doesn't occur to me to even walk into a clothing store, until my "wardrobe" gets so shabby I start feeling mildly embarrassed by it. And that's exactly where I had arrived. I was wearing the same four or five shirts to work every week, and they were beginning to fade from too many washings. My jeans were starting to get brittle, and knee and/or crotch holes were but a few days away. I bought a pair at Target last weekend (with my underwear on) but I needed a few more. So I reluctantly took a couple hundred bucks out of the bank on Saturday, and hit the outlets with Toney and her mother.

I probably would've put it off a month or two more if I didn't work with a couple of guys who, when they're not yelling and berating their employees, critique people's fashion sense and grooming. These men walk around with their chests puffed out, and their anger barely in check, but they dish the dirt in private like a couple of old ladies at the beauty shop. I've heard them say things like, "He looks like he packed his suitcase out of a hamper," and

"Her shirt has never seen an iron." One of these guys presses his jeans, I shit you not. I know I've been the focus of their ridicule for many things, and I don't need to give them more ammo by letting my shirts lose some of their vibrancy.

The outlets in Stroudsburg, PA are better than most of the other outlet "malls" I've visited. It's still a three-ring circus, and a lot of the stores are not really outlets at all, but as these things go, this one is pretty good. It's huge and always teeming with people. Buses from God-knows-where continuously deposit more and more over-caffeinated shoppers into the mix, and parking spots have almost monetary value. It's like Disneyland, or visiting a Major League ballpark, without all the pesky distraction of fun. We got there when the place opened at 10 am in an attempt to minimize the pain, and it actually worked for a while.

Things started out well. I bought a few shirts at the Gap store for ten bucks a piece, which I felt good about. They would've cost fifty each at a real Gap in a mall somewhere. This is why I say these outlets are pretty decent; you can find some real deals there. We continued on and I picked up a few more things here and there, and the crowds were not yet suffocating. But eventually my mother-in-law could contain herself no more and started wandering off by herself. So we were forced to do a lot of standing around waiting on her, lest we get separated for good (I'm not exactly sure why that would've been a bad thing, but I was told that it would be). She doesn't believe in starting at one end of the mall and working your way to the other end systematically. She likes to bounce around with no rhyme or reason. She's like a kid in a toy store, just going from one thing to another. It was making me crazy. She threw my whole shopping rhythm off, and things started going downhill fast.

During all the waiting around, buses were continuously spewing forth large groups of space-taking shoppers, and the place started to get crazy. I got the feeling that most of the people were from New York, based on their accents and attitudes. My level of irritation and blood pressure began to creep upwards. At one point I was in a store that sold lamps and household crap, and I found a desk clock that I wanted. There were butch women all around me at the checkout for some reason, and one of them dropped a giant fart bomb. It smelled like an outhouse in there. It was absolutely disgusting, and nobody else acted like they could even smell it. I pulled my shirt up over my nose, paid for the damn clock, and power-walked out. Standing around smelling lesbian gas is not what I had in mind when I got out of bed on Saturday morning.

We tried to soldier on to the end, but we finally gave it up about two-thirds of the way into it. It was like some kind of Moroccan street fair at that point. It was literally hard to walk, and you had to jockey for position whenever you found something of interest. And some members of the population smell better than others, I'm sad to say. Now I know what they mean by "the great unwashed." Screw that. I don't care if they're giving shit away; nothing's worth that hassle. So we trudged back to the car and gave up our premium real estate in the parking lot to some lucky bastard, and headed home.

I wish I had time to go into it now, but my mother-in-law launched into one of her patented diatribes on the drive home. It was one of her better efforts, I must say, and I'll write about it next time. I swear to God I feel like I'm living in a real-life sitcom sometimes…

February 28, 2001

Besides wildly exaggerated characters created by professional writers to amuse us on television, I've never encountered anyone like my mother in law. I don't have the energy or desire to try to paint the whole picture for you here, that would require a whole other website (is crazyasfuck.com taken?), but I'd like tell you about a couple of recent incidents that are a pretty good representation of the whole experience.

When we were driving home from our shopping trip on Saturday, conversation turned to money and this sent her off on one of her loud and lengthy diatribes. Whenever she slips into this mode, which is often, she takes on the tone of a person giving a speech. On Saturday she once again began emoting as if she were addressing an auditorium full of people — in our Toyota. The thesis of this particular sermon: Life is too short for hard work and ambition.

She told us she never bought into all that "responsibility bullshit", and insinuated we've been conned because we own a house and make car payments and go to work every day. She said she'd rather live in the cheapest apartment she can find, drive "shit cars", and not owe anyone anything. That way, she said, she can blow her money and not be tied to any one job, and "be able to leave town at a moment's notice." That last part really made me laugh. Yeah, she's quite the rambler.

She said blowing money is the one thing in life that makes her happy, and she's not going to "waste" her dollars on a mortgage "and all that bullshit". And, naturally, we shouldn't either. She's the type that thinks everyone should lead their lives exactly as she does, and any deviation from that is a judgment of her. Don't judge the judge, goddamnit. Of course, the concepts of investment and stability and self-control are completely foreign to her, so there's no point in arguing about it. It's best just to weather the storm, and move on.

Toney did ask her if she ever gets jealous of other people, and their houses and savings accounts and retirement plans. She spat out an angry, "No!" with a look of complete contempt on her face. She admitted she'd like a nice house, but only if somebody would give it to her — a telling remark. She said she wasn't interested in something if it required a lot of effort to acquire. And she said this in a bragging, self-satisfied tone, as if she were an elderly Thomas Edison reflecting on a life's work.

Of course, all of this is a load of crap. Toney's mother is jealous of people who've lived responsibly — like my parents — and she hates them for it. They're just rich bastards, and she'd like to see them all run over by busses simultaneously. She's one of the angriest and bitterest people I've ever known. It's true she's lived a life dedicated to instant gratification, but not because of some well thought-out and agonized-over worldview, like she'll tell you now. She's spoiled, like a kid. She's more than just a little lazy, and has a deep-seated sense of entitlement. These lofty ideals of hers, the dropping out of society and avoiding the rat race and all that garbage, are justifications arrived at after the fact. One of her favorite tricks is to re-write history, and that's exactly what she's doing here.

This stuff used to drive me crazy, but after ten years it's now mostly amusing. Some of it's downright hilarious. What mother lectures her child for being ambitious? That's just good comedy. I wish I had it on tape.

March 3, 2001

— My mother in law has now proclaimed to Toney that she will never go anywhere with us again, as long as I'm driving. She said she was completely mortified last Saturday, and was convinced I would flip the vehicle at several points. I find this to be highly entertaining, of course. But please note how she's turned a simple half-day of shopping into a weeklong festival of bitterness. Yes, this is my life.

— Yesterday at Wendy's some guy dropped his fries, made a quick maneuver to try to scoop them off the floor, and blew the ass out his pants. Giant white vertical rip. I laughed for ten minutes.

March 5, 2001

No work today because of the snow. It started coming down yesterday around noon, and it's not supposed to stop until some time tomorrow, so they didn't open the office today. The pinheads on TV have been saying we could get as much as thirty inches before it's over. I find that hard to believe, but what do I know? It's certainly got everyone whipped into a frenzy, that much is for sure.

I went to the grocery store yesterday morning and it was like a visit to the Soviet Union. Long lines, people fighting over loaves of bread, white skin and red lips, the whole deal. It was pretty grim. I was getting coffee, but everybody else seemed to be stocking a bomb shelter. How long do these people think we'll be snowed in? Even if we get the thirty inches, everything will be back to normal by Thursday. I think it's more than just a little nutty to rush out and buy a month's worth of groceries, because of snow. My only concession to the hysteria: two cases of Yuengling instead of one. You don't gamble with the necessities.

I'm really glad they decided not to open the office today. I would've tried to go in even if the snow was up to the windows. It's a matter of pride. If one other person had made it and I didn't, the locals would've busted my ass and called me California Boy for a week. I can't have that. So I would've attempted to make it even if it meant tunneling my way in. There are some things worth dying for.

March 7, 2001

Of course the Storm of the Century didn't quite materialize. We did get eleven or twelve inches of snow over a couple of days, which isn't insignificant, but it's a long way from the thirty inches they were holding over our heads this weekend. By the time I left work yesterday, the roads were completely clear and the world was back to normal. I bet there's a lot of people thinking, "Damn, what am I going to do with all this milk and bread?" I read yesterday that some guy from The Weather Channel was doing a report from NYC, and a bunch of people turned on him and were yelling "Liar!!", and pelting him with snowballs. I think people are getting a little tired of all the false alarms.

But enough about the weather. I feel like a senior citizen. Next I'll start telling you what I had for lunch.

Toney talked to our old next-door neighbor from California yesterday. She's the one who told her about the field of toddler shit I wrote about a few weeks ago. Anyway, she was going on and on about how many improvements the new owners of our old house have made. For some reason this irritates me. I feel like it's a judgment of us. Hell, we did a lot while we were there too. We put on a new roof, put up gutters, a new garage door, had it painted, re-did the ceilings, painted the interior walls, had the flooring replaced in the kitchen, etc. But in suburbia I guess you're only as good as your last home improvement. Plus it's worth pointing out that the new owner is an airline pilot. I have a feeling he doesn't have to roll coins a few days before payday, like I had to do a few times when I lived in that SoCal "paradise."

Sometimes when I blow my nose snot comes out of my left tear duct. Always the left one. What would cause snot to come out of a person's eye? Am I dying? Or should I just adjust the pressure a little?

I'm thinking about creating a series of mystery novels starring Charlie Daniels as a crime solver. He travels the country in a tour bus with his fiddle and hat, and solves murder mysteries. What do you think? Heck, maybe I could even pitch it as a TV series. CBS would probably buy it. I'm going to trust you guys not to steal this golden idea from me.

I'm taking Friday off and my friend Steve and I are driving to Pottsville, PA to tour the Yuengling plant. It's the oldest brewery in the US, built in 1829. How cool will that be? I can't wait. This is my Jerusalem.

March 12, 2001

I'm sure you've seen those nitwits on television who've just won 25 or 50 million dollars in a state lottery, smiling like jack o' lanterns and proudly proclaiming they're going to continue working — pressing other people's pants in a suffocating gray laundromat, or some such hell — because that's "who they are". I was thinking about that on my drive home Friday, from a great day away from work, and my long-held contention that those people are obviously crazy or incredibly stupid was further cemented in my mind. There's so much to see and do, how could you choose to sit on the sidelines?

My friend Steve and I have been talking about touring the Yuengling plant for a few months, and we finally just circled a date on the calendar and did it. We decided to go on a weekday, because the brewery doesn't really operate on weekends and we wanted to witness it in its full glory. In case you're not familiar with Yuengling, it's a regional, family-owned brewery that's operated continuously since 1829 (they made ice cream and non-alcoholic brews during prohibition), and they produce one of the best beers in the world, Yuengling Lager. My liver's had its hands full filtering these products since I moved to Pennsylvania a little over a year ago, and I've wanted to visit their birthplace since day one.

I drove to Steve's house in Danville, and we had an early lunch at a cool little bar/restaurant in the downtown area, and hit the road for Pottsville to make the 1:30 tour. It's only about forty miles from Steve's house, and it wasn't long before we saw the giant black letters that spell Yuengling on the side of a hill overlooking the crumbling town. I felt like a kid on the way to an amusement park, catching the first glimpse of the roller coaster peaking up above the trees. I think my redneck roots even resurfaced for a second and caused me to involuntarily blurt out, "Hell yeah!"

My first impression, after we parked and started walking around, is that the building is extremely old. I mean really old. Like Independence Hall old. There are ancient brick sidewalks around the towering brewery and some of the windows (the ones not facing the town) are busted, and appear to have been that way since Strom Thurmond was in a playpen. The foundation has gaping holes in it in places, and the glass is wavy. It's like something out of Dickens.

We were a few minutes early, so we went into the gift shop to wait. Imagine any item big enough to emblazon with a company logo, and chances are they had it there. I saw fingernail clippers, aprons, yardsticks, playing cards, and a thousand other little things. And they had big things as well, like patio umbrellas, neon signs, afghans(?!), and a giant inner tube designed for sledding. It was far too much to take in before the guide stuck her head in the room and told everyone to please follow her. We'd just have to come back after the tour.

She took us down the hall to a small bar, originally built in the 1930's for employees. They used to be allowed to knock back beers on their breaks and lunches there! Not anymore; now it's just used for tours and the company Christmas party. Some douchebag undoubtedly ruined it for everyone by getting drunk and falling into one of the brewing vats, or getting an arm hung up in a bottle capper or something. Assholes are always ruining it for the rest of us. I should've asked her about that, but there were too many people. I felt a little disappointed that it wasn't a more intimate group, being a weekday and all, but what are you going to do?

After she gave us a brief history of the brewery, she took us to the brew house. Really cool. In addition to the expected stainless steel vats, there's a stained glass ceiling and giant colorful murals on the walls. Workers were transferring the contents of one of the vats into another, and the smell was almost overpowering. It was like they had a huge beer-filled humidifier going.

From there she took us outside to show us the aging facilities. When the brewery was built in the early 1800's they dug a u-shaped cave deep into the mountain behind it for this purpose, but they stopped using it about thirty years ago. Now they just have a big building beside the brew house. The cave is still there, she said, but they don't allow the tours to enter it anymore because the floors are too slippery. Again, some asshole undoubtedly ruined it by hurtling to the ground, completely baffled by surfaces that aren't absolutely dry.

Following a quick pass through the bottling/canning facility, we all piled back into the bar for the ceremonial tasting of the product. I was disappointed that they only allowed you two cups each, but it was better than nothing. I selected the Premium Light (because it was the only one I'd never had) and the Lord Chesterfield Ale. Both were very tasty, indeed. As everyone sat around sipping their golden elixirs, people started asking the guide some questions. I should say one woman started asking the guide some questions. She wanted to know, among other things, where they get the water they use, why they don't increase the use of returnable bottles to cut down on waste, and (in a rather accusatory tone) why none of the Yuengling women have ever ran the brewery. Pain—In—The—Ass.

After we were pleasantly buzzed, they set us free in the gift shop again. I don't think there's anything coincidental about that. I spent $25 on stuff, and Steve plunked down considerably more. The tab would've probably been a lot less without the beakers of beer they served us. But what the hell, now I have a cool black Yuengling license plate for the front of my truck, and a couple of new shirts.

When we were walking back to the car we noticed we smelled like the vats of thick churning beer sludge in the brew house, and it clung to us for hours. When I opened a bottle of lager on Saturday night, the smell made me a little queasy for a second. But I quickly got over it. Very quickly, in fact.

I'll write about the rest of the day next time. Steve and I visited the mysterious town of Centralia, and a hospital pathology lab after we left the brewery, for one of the more surreal afternoons of my life.

March 15, 2001

Centralia used to be just another small town in the middle of Pennsylvania. It had a town square, schools, businesses, a mayor, local eccentrics, and all the other things you'd expect. Unfortunately, it's far from just another small town today. In fact, it's barely a town at all. It doesn't even appear on all the maps anymore.

In May of 1962, the city burned some trash in an open pit, like they had done many times before, and somehow ignited a fire in a mineshaft that runs underneath the town. In that part of the world there's a lot of slow-burning anthracite coal in the ground and, amazingly enough, the fire's still burning almost forty years later.

Attempts to extinguish it were unsuccessful, and very costly, so they eventually abandoned the idea. Until the 1980's, folks didn't think too much about it. It burned deep under the ground, and they saw little evidence of it. It was something they joked about, when they spoke of it at all. But then people started getting sick, and tests determined that, because of the fire, harmful gasses were coming out of the ground into people's houses. Also, the main road through town eventually collapsed into a huge sinkhole, as the fire moved closer to the surface. Smoke, and sometimes actual flames, rose from the ground in spots. The government came in and did a bunch of studies, and concluded that it would cost $663 million to put the fire out. So they came up with an alternate plan: they'd buy every home and business in the town, so everyone could move away from the problem. That would only cost $42 million.

And so, people started leaving in droves and the feds tore their houses down as soon as the moving trucks pulled away from the curb. Little by little, the once-bustling community withered away. Today there are only a handful of die-hards still living there, some in single homes that used to be part of a group of row houses — tall and skinny and strange looking, with supports on the sides so the walls don't fall down. Predictably, some of the ones who've stayed (depending on what article you're reading, it's either 24 or 42 people now), consider the whole affair to be a giant government conspiracy. I don't know about that, but I do know it's a pretty cool place to visit.

Since Steve and I were in the neighborhood, touring the Yuengling brewery in Pottsville, we decided to check out Centralia on our way home. When we pulled into "town" I thought we'd made some kind of mistake. There's almost literally nothing left; it's just a huge open field, with an occasional house here and there. I had it pictured as sort of a ghost town, like on TV. I didn't know a lot of the story at that point, I did my research after the fact, and it hadn't occurred to me that they'd torn down all the buildings. The weird part is, even though the houses and businesses are gone, the streets remain. There's block after block of empty lots, with random sets of steps leading to nothing. We saw an old abandoned playground, and fire hydrants wrapped in plastic. The street signs are gone too, and it reminded me a little of a giant abandoned campground.

We drove around, but we never saw evidence of an old downtown or anything like that. Maybe it's gone too. (I want to do some more exploring next time I go, maybe as soon as this weekend.) But we did find a hillside, next to an old cemetery that was smoking like a bastard. Oh, we had to get a closer look at this. So we parked and walked up the road towards the big clouds. It was really bizarre. It looked like a war zone up there. Dead trees were laying everywhere, bleached white from the heat, and the ground was black and smoking. I read that at one point flames and smoke were coming up around the headstones in the cemetery. Oh man, I wish I could've seen that! What kind of karma is that, to be burned up in the grave?

Beer bottles were laying everywhere. People obviously came up there to socialize. We kept walking and the smoke kept getting thicker. It smelled like sulfur, and we tried not to breathe in much of it — you know, since it's poisonous and all. And then we saw something I'll never forget. There was carpeting, and a goddmamn couch at the top of the hill. Steve later found out that the smoking hillside is a popular place to take a date! People probably had sex up there, with coal smoke coming up around them. And if that wasn't enough, there were giant clam shells laying everywhere. People were eating seafood. They'd held a clambake! It was all so incredibly bizarre.

If you ever get the chance to visit this place, I strongly urge you to do so. I was more amazed by Centralia than I was the Yuengling plant, and that's saying something. Like I mentioned, I may go back on Sunday to see the sunken road and do some more general exploring. What a trip!

As if that weren't enough excitement for one day, we stopped by the hospital where Steve's wife Myra works, before I hit the road for home. Myra's a doctor, specifically a doctor of pathology. On our way in Steve showed me a sign on a door that said something like, "Attention Funeral Directors: All Remains Must Be Signed Out By Hospital Personnel Before They Can Be Removed From the Premises." What the hell?! Once inside, Steve kept urging Myra to show me something disgusting. She finally sighed, like she'd been through this many times before, and signaled for us to follow her.

We went into a small lab and she showed us a stack of plastic containers full of yellowish, cloudy liquid and clumps of some kind of vile grossness. Steve asked her what they were, and she bent down to read the labels, and replied casually, "Colon... colon... colon... placenta... colon." The colons were cancerous, and had recently been removed from patients. I asked her about some big globs of yellow crap in one of the containers, and she told me it was an especially fatty colon. That did it for me. I was done. See ya next time, sports fans! But Steve started trying to talk her into letting us go in the morgue. I was a little apprehensive about that but, of course, I would've gone. Unfortunately(?), she couldn't get the key and we missed out on that particular experience.

But, what a day. Giant vats of the best beer in the world, smoking hillsides, and fatty colons encased in Tupperware. These are the things dreams are made of. If the planets ever align and I win the lottery, I can assure you I'm not going to continue to work. I probably won't even go in and take down my Harry Potter calendar. This world is full of amazing stuff, and I want to see as much of it as I can. There's a Disneyland around every corner, if you just take the time to find it.

March 19, 2001

— I was coming back from lunch one day last week, walking in the parking lot at work, and felt the ground vibrating beneath me. As I continued on I could feel the bass-thump of somebody's car stereo threatening to interfere with the workings of my heart. I mean the thing was cranked. It kept getting louder and louder until I reached a huge Dodge pickup with some guy sitting behind the wheel, and I was finally able to make out what he was blasting inside the cab: "Shambala" by Three Dog Night. Some men just need to rock.

— Speaking of trucks, I saw a Ford pickup the other day that had big letters stenciled on its tailgate that read, "Built with tools, not chopsticks." Not to be overly analytical, but that doesn't even make sense. I'm not an expert, but I'm not aware of vehicles being built anywhere in the world with eating utensils.

— I also saw, on another of my lunch breaks last week (I take a lot of breaks), that somebody had a child's safety seat in their car that was completely covered in Dale Earnhardt logos and likenesses. I'm not sure I'd feel too safe with my kid strapped into a Dale Earnhardt car seat. Did they also get him the Matthew Perry sip cup?

— I read in an obituary for Morton Downey Jr. that he wrote the '60s surf hit "Wipeout." Can that possibly be true? How bizarre is that? I'm imagining him shirtless and on a surfboard, with his facial warts tanned bronze, cig a-danglin'. And I don't really want to think these thoughts.

— This is an actual bio written by a woman who was one year behind me in high school, at classmates.com:

widowed,has four children i like to hear from my old classmates. i really haven't see much of anyone since i have served in the us army. i presently going to school to be registered nurse. please contact me.

And this is one of her fondest memories:

learning to be a real solider and to represent my country good usa well

No, she wasn't the valedictorian, but that was a good one!

— Saturday night Toney and I caught half of an episode of Jeopardy, and one of the categories was Hee Haw. She looked on in complete disgust as I ripped through the category, cranking off instantaneous correct answers left and right. I think she particularly enjoyed the part where I screamed, "Oh come on! Radio station KORN! KORN!! Are you stupid?!"

March 22, 2001

— I know our chain is probably being yanked, but there are finally some signs of spring here in the northeast. Almost the entire snow-pack has melted away, and the days are getting longer and warmer. It won't be long before I get to trade in the snow shovel for a lawn mower, and start bitching about something new. But we'll be getting a big bonus during this year's season of renewal that I'll never complain about: my mother in law is moving back to Reno! She leaves in the middle of April, abandoning her experimental east coast expansion of Project Bitterness and returning to her beloved hometown in the desert (aka The Worst Place on Earth). Yes, it might still snow a few more times this year, but every shovel full will bring me that much closer to that wonderful, glorious eighteenth day of April. I swear, if I were a pussy-boy I'd break down and weep.

— I read that Spike Lee has written an article claiming that Babe Ruth was actually a black man. I'll withhold sarcastic comments until after I've had a chance to read the piece, but this oughta be good.

— Yet another promise to myself that I recently broke is to never return to Boston Market. I went there for lunch earlier this week, and it was a fiasco. I ordered a meatloaf sandwich, mashed potatoes, and a drink — seven bucks. Shit! And there was so much ketchup on the sandwich that I had it halfway to my elbows within seconds. I finally ended up eating it with a knife and fork, then going into the bathroom for a scrub down. And, after all that maintenance, I was still hungry on my drive back to work. I also discovered a nickel-sized ketchup stain on my jacket later that day. I can't imagine why they're having financial problems.

— I also recently picked up a little booklet at a flea market called 2001 Southern Superstitions. Because I care about your well-being, I'd like to share a few of the entries with you here. You can thank me later, when you're happy, healthy, and beautiful.

If your cornbread is rough, your husband's face will be rough.

If you cut your hair in March, you will lose a horse.

Go behind a door and eat a chicken foot to become beautiful.

If you get the front of your dress wet while washing your clothes, your husband will be a drunkard.

If you hold an apple in your armpit until it is warm and then eat it, your sweetheart will love you.

If a girl wears a wasp nest in her clothing, her lover will love her more deeply.

Eat a dozen onions before you go to bed, to become beautiful.

If a dog steps on your pulled tooth, you will have a dog tooth.

If you cut your toenails on Friday, you will never have a toothache.

If you cut a lock of a dog's hair and put it under your pillow, you will dream what the dog has dreamed.

If you drop a broom while sweeping, you will get new carpet.

If you are troubled by witches it is a good idea to sleep with a meal sifter over your face.

Now, go do the right thing.

March 25, 2001

I looked at myself in the mirror earlier this week and I had giant black circles under my eyes. For a second I thought I was looking at a poster of Frank Torre. Dear god, when did this happen to me? I may have to invest in some of that Victoria Principal eye cream. It's really sad, when you think about it.

On Friends Thursday night they were playing a game where they each had to write down all fifty states within six minutes. Ross had 49, and spent the rest of the episode losing his shit over not being able to come up with the last one. (Joey had 56.) Anyway, after it went off Toney and I tried it and we both had 48 — the same 48. How weird is that? Ten years together and we're in such perfect sync that we've both blocked out the existence of Connecticut and Minnesota. Now that's love.

March 28, 2001

— I almost had a bad wreck yesterday. I was driving home from work, on a heavily traveled stretch of road, when some old dried-up apple sculpture of a man pulled out in front of me. He was stopped at a stop sign on a side street that crosses the one I was on, and for no apparent reason suddenly started out across traffic, moving at roughly three miles an hour. Time stood still for a split second as my brain tried to process the impossible events taking place before me, then I stomped on the brakes. There was screeching and smoking and fishtailing, and all that good stuff, followed by a lot of profanity and waving of arms. By the looks of her, it's possible the woman in the passenger seat of the old man's car was already dead, but if she wasn't she came very close to being delivered to her maker by a Toyota pickup truck. Man, you gotta play defense during every waking hour.

— Have you seen that commercial for a Barbie that comes with a cat that pisses? I'm not joking. It has a little toy litter box and everything. I'm thinking they should go the extra mile and do a cross-promotion with Play-Doh, and get some cat turds going for the kiddies too. And maybe a little yapping dog to eat the turds out of the litter box. If they're going to open up the world of pet waste, why not take it to its logical conclusion?

— I heard a radio commercial today advertising Easter services at a church in Wilkes-Barre. First of all, since when do churches run radio ads? Isn't that for car dealers and Mountain Dew and stuff? I thought it was a bit odd, but when I heard the pastor start talking I forgot all about it. The man had a major speech impediment, and I simply couldn't believe my ears. He was asking people to join him for a "celebwation of the glowy of Chwist." I shit you not, he repeatedly said "Chwist." I'm going to try to get it on tape.

April 2, 2001

— Yesterday was opening day for baseball season and the Cincinnati Reds didn't play, which is blasphemy. The Reds are the oldest team in the majors and, for as long as I can remember, it has been tradition that they open each new season. When I was a kid I used to cut school to watch the Reds play on television on opening day. Or Opening Day, as I thought of it back then. I remember the principal of my Junior High calling me down to his office and asking me where I had disappeared to after lunch the previous afternoon, and I just shrugged and said, "Opening Day." Surprisingly, that seemed to satisfy him. He apparently understood priorities, and let me go without even a slap on the wrist. Unfortunately, opening day doesn't produce the same kind of magic as it once did. Now it's just two random teams that ESPN thinks will be good for ratings. Tradition be damned. Unless it's marketable, Major League Baseball doesn't have much respect for tradition anymore. Interleague play is proof of that. I doubt there are many kids sneaking off from school to watch baseball games these days, which is sad enough. But some of the reasons for it make me sick.

— The windshield wiper blades on my truck recently disintegrated and I was left with two naked metal rods that waved back and forth and cut circular grooves into the glass. I wanted to just take the truck somewhere and pay somebody to fix the problem, but I knew Toney would make fun of my lack of mechanical abilities. So I got some replacement blades and tried to install them myself. I spent roughly a half-hour on the project and got nowhere. I was completely stumped, even though I had directions to consult. Step one in the four step process baffled me, and I quickly became enraged. So, screw it. Saturday I took it to a garage and asked the guy how much he'd charge me to install the blades I'd bought. He chuckled and said he'd put them on free of charge, the implication being he couldn't in good conscious take money for something so incredibly simple. I'm pretty certain I detected a trace of pity in his voice as well. I guess I should just get it over with and box up my genitals now. I'm sure the recall notice will be arriving soon.

— Since we moved here a year ago, the McCrory's store close to our house has had signs up announcing they're going out of business. Total Liquidation. Store Closing. These had been up for a solid year, but have now been replaced with others that say, Grand Opening. Makes perfect sense to me. Heck, I'm just excited we're getting a new business in town.

— I've been noticing a commercial for a bizarre little toy called Johnny Apple Bot. It looks like a red apple with a face, and it sings and dances and spews pseudo-hip catch phrases like, "Don't go there!" and "You go girl!" Why would anyone purchase such an item? People who act like that are avoided and/or beaten. The fact that it's a battery-powered piece of fruit being obnoxious doesn't change much, really. What's next, a racist, lip-smacking pear? A whiny onion saddled with self-loathing? A box of judgmental raisins? We've come a long way since the invention of the Kung Fu Grip, I'm telling ya.

April 8, 2001

— Since the in-laws will be moving back to the luscious green paradise that is Sparks, Nevada (aka America's Butthole) in a few days, Toney thought it would be a good idea to take them out for a nice meal before they leave town. So, this morning we went to brunch at a rather upscale joint called Genetti Manor. It was a buffet, and it turned out to be pretty nice. The food was plentiful and good, the people friendly, and the dining room spacious. Of course, this drove my mother-in-law absolutely crazy. She's not completely satisfied with a situation unless she has something to bitch about, and this place denied her that pleasure. She was miserable because she wasn't miserable. You can try to figure that out if you'd like; I've stopped trying. In retrospect, I know we should've taken them to some crowded, overpriced place full of uppity snobs. I guess we're just not very thoughtful. We should've been more attentive to her needs.

Even though Toney's mother had little to bitch about at breakfast, I provided her with some relief by driving there. I mentioned a few weeks ago that she had made the proclamation, as if addressing a joint session of Congress, that she would never go anywhere with us again, as long as I'm doing the driving. She said my driving terrified her, which I found highly amusing. I'm not exactly Robbie Knievel on the roadways. Originally we were going to take separate vehicles, but I guess she realized how ridiculous that was, and agreed to ride with us.

Everything went OK until we merged onto the interstate — those crazy, fast-moving Scranton freeways. Unless I was in the right lane, moving at 55 mph or lower, with a football field of space between us and any other car on the road, she would gasp and throw a death-grip on whatever was handy. When we came up behind a man who probably fought in the Spanish-American War, traveling at a brisk 45, I passed him, as any normal functioning adult would. Well, I'm surprised she didn't shit her pants. She began flailing her arms and gasping for air, like she was riding in the cockpit of a Blue Angel. When we finally got to the restaurant, she was the color of typing paper. It made my day. I'm one crazy left-lane-driving mofo.

And it's not like this woman is some meek and timid individual, either. She's constantly arguing with people in stores and restaurants, and threatening to kick somebody's ass. I've heard her tell more than one person, "The last thing you're going to see are my headlights, bitch." That's one of her favorites. And I personally witnessed her being barred for life from a Reno restaurant, for relentlessly harassing a waitress — and that's but one place of business where she'll be arrested if she ever steps foot back on the property. This is no delicate flower I'm talking about here. Again, please feel free to try to figure it out if you'd like.

— I know it must seem like I'm making some of this shit up, but I swear on the Velvet Underground box set it's all true.

I work in an office with a massive warehouse attached to it. I don't know many of the people who work on "the floor", except for a few of the managers, and one of them has been filling me in on every little minute detail of his pending new car purchase. Whenever he sees me his eyes light up and quickly makes his way over to begin telling me about all the new problems he's encountered with the incredibly drawn-out transaction. He seems like a nice enough guy, and I don't really mind listening to him, but he reminds me of Cliff from Cheers. He fancies himself an expert in most fields, and injects technical terms and stats into his speech whenever possible.

On Thursday I was walking through the warehouse and he came over as usual and said, "So, did you hear that the American penis is getting shorter?"

"Pardon?"

"It's true." he said. "The average length of the American penis has been 6.2 inches for years, but has dropped to 5.8 during the last decade."

"Does it have anything to do with the internet?" I asked.

He ignored that and went on to tell me that even at the revised length, he came up short. "I'm only hitting at about five and a half inches," he said.

"Well…I'm not sure what to say about that…" I said.

"My ex used to tell me I was huge, but I think she just did it to make me get into the sex more.…One of the reasons we broke up is because she lied all the time," he said.

"You broke up with your fiancee because she said you had a big dick?"

"Well, there's more to it than that." he said.

"Sounds complicated," I offered.

"You don't know the half of it, brother," he said.

There's a Disneyland around every corner.

April 11, 2001

— Yesterday when I was buying a sandwich in the cafeteria at work, the cashier suddenly became excited and said, "Oh look, a new quarter! I haven't seen this one yet. North Carolina....it has an airplane on the back for some reason." "Yeah, that would be Kitty Hawk. Right?" I answered, trying to fake at least a mild interest in the subject. She looked at me like I'd just said something that made absolutely no sense, like I was a mental patient on the loose. When she saw that I wasn't making a joke, her face wadded up into an ugly ball and I'm almost sure I heard a faint grinding noise coming from inside her head.

— Speaking of work…they have full-time 24/7 security there, with lots of uniformed guards and all the trimmings. When you leave the building these guys go through all your shit to make sure you're not walking off with somebody's hard drive or something. Most of the guards are older retired men who don't take it too seriously. They joke around and laugh, and basically behave like normal, civilized human beings. But there are a handful who act like they're protecting national security secrets at The Pentagon. They never smile, and refuse to even say Good Morning. Oh no, that would portray an image of weakness. These guys can't afford to be distracted by the niceties and courtesies of the outside world. They're highly trained law enforcement officers, you see, who must constantly be on the lookout for suspicious activities among the hardened criminals who pass them each day. I'd bet real money they constantly badger their bosses to get them some of those cool Secret Service mics, so they can start talking into their sleeves. What a bunch of douches. And why do people who act like this always have moustaches? Always. There are no exceptions.

April 16, 2001

I looked in the mirror a few days ago and there was a strange mutant creature staring back at me. Sort of a mixture of Walter Mondale and Gabe Kaplan, which meant that it was time to get another haircut, as well as a bunch of other stuff that I can't do much about.

I was off from work on Friday, so I trucked my sad ass down to the family-oriented hair maintenance center early in the morning. I wanted to get there around the time they opened, so I might not have to wait so long. But it didn't work out: the chirpy teenage girl at the desk informed me it would be at least an hour wait. Screw that. I always have to hang around that place for an inordinate amount of time, and I'm not doing it again. I decided to go hunting for a real barber shop.

I quickly found one, and had to park in a metered spot. I had no change, and wasn't clear on whether you have to pay on holidays, or whether Good Friday was even considered a holiday. I decided to risk it, but it made me a little uneasy. When I stepped into the barber shop, I saw that nearly every seat in the waiting area was occupied and there was only one barber working. And when he heard the door open he whipped his head around, and shot me a dirty look. Apparently the man was having a bad day. A bad hair day. So, screw him. I'm not risking a $35 parking ticket for the privilege of having an embittered small-town barber with a laughable comb-over give me a haircut. I turned around and left.

I started doing a mental inventory of the town, trying to remember if I'd seen a striped barber pole anywhere. I seemed to recall seeing one on the front of a cigar store a few blocks away. I remembered it because Toney had said the place looks creepy on more than one occasion. And, although I'd never dwelled on it, I now realized my mind had had a problem processing the fact that there was a barber pole hanging on the front of a cigar store. I quickly decided to give it a shot.

It's an old house that had been transformed into a place of business years ago. It looked like somebody lived upstairs, and the cigar store was on the main floor. There was indeed a striped pole mounted to the side of the building, so I parked and got out to investigate. When I walked up the front steps I saw a piece of cardboard taped to the inside of the window with "Barber on Duty" scribbled on it in ballpoint, among several neon signs and ads for various brands of cigars. I heard a motor revving nearby, and looked around and saw a group of men messing with a motorcycle in the side yard.

When I went inside there was a wooden Indian in full headdress standing guard by a door at the end of a short, dark hallway. Inside the door were several giant humidors, a lot of dark wood paneling, some glass cases full of smoking paraphernalia, a few dusty-looking rugs, an old woman....and a barber chair. "Here to see the barber?" the woman asked immediately, obviously noticing the Kaplanesque load of hair piled on top of my head. I considered making a run for it, but gulped and said, "yeah." "I'll go get him," she said, "he's working on his motorcycle."

Holy shit!

While I waited, a giant bald guy in a black leather jacket came in and took a couple boxes of expensive cigars, with a promise of "dropping a check off later." "No, problem! Have a nice day!" the old woman responded. What kind of place is this?!, I thought to myself. Nothing seemed to add up. Finally a very old man in a baby-blue smock came in, smelling of gasoline. "Have a seat, sir," he directed me.

After some introductory pleasantries, he asked me how I wanted it cut. I told him short, with the clippers, and this seemed to please him. He fired up a large vibrating metal box that had apparently served as clippers in days gone by, and started scraping it across my skull. It felt like the jagged edge of a broken tree branch, and was making a troubling clickety-clack sound. "What kind of work do you do?" he asked, absent-mindedly. After I told him, he immediately rattled off the names of several people I've never heard of, who supposedly work there too. They probably retired in 1978.

As our conversation continued, his speech became more and more colorful. He injected the word "goddamn" wherever possible, and added a few "shits" and "assholes" for contrast. I asked him how many years he'd been cutting hair, and he said, "Fifty-two goddamn years. A hell of long time, if you ask me." And I'm almost sure I saw sparks fly off the box as it moved close to my right eye — which was especially troublesome considering the man was apparently marinated in gasoline.

But I started doing the math: fifty-two years. That means he started in 1949. Who was president then, Truman? Incredible. Mickey Mantle was still in the minor leagues, and the Korean War was getting ready to crank up. Men wore suits and hats all the time. Television was as new as DVDs are now. "I've cut a lot of heads," he said, "I wish I'd put a goddamn dime away for every head I've cut." This guy's a walking, talking, hair-clipping historical monument.

And in just a few minutes, he was done. He held up a mirror so I could approve his work, which I did automatically. But, secretly, my heart started pounding. My head was shaved! In no time Gabe Kaplan had been replaced with Timothy McVeigh. Shit! Without a doubt, one of the worst haircuts I've ever had. I looked like a big retarded stock-boy.

But why sweat the details? I'm not going to win any beauty contests, even if Vidal Sassoon himself cuts my hair. Yes, I might have found myself a barber.

April 19, 2001

— From the I Simply Can't Believe It file comes this little nugget of ridiculousness. After six months, the in-laws finally packed it in and moved back to The Worst Place on Earth (aka Sparks, Nevada). They left on Sunday morning, and I actually spent the day feeling a little empty and sad. I could've never predicted this reaction. I figured I'd be dancing and celebrating, perhaps even indulging in the purchase of a paper Chinese dragon to make the party complete. But I felt strangely disoriented and not at all interested in a celebration. I've chronicled here how big a pain in the ass my mother-in-law can be, and there's no doubt she's a lunatic, but I'd gotten used to her presence. All day Sunday it felt weird not to have her sitting in our living room with a large tumbler of gin, ripping everyone a new asshole. It threw my whole rhythm off. I think I'm actually gonna miss that crazy woman.

— Another trip I hope to make in the near future is to Greensboro, NC for a reunion-of-sorts with some folks I used to work with at a record store there. It's been about ten or twelve years since we all drifted apart, and we're trying to get together for one more night of long-neck Rolling Rocks and conversation at the greatest beer bar in the land, College Hill Sundries. I'm really looking forward to it. My four years in Greensboro was a magical time. It was a period of newly-realized freedom, an extraordinary group of friends, always interesting situations, and lots of fun. Some of the best people I've ever known I met at Peaches in Greensboro. I can't wait to see them all again.

April 25, 2001

— The day after Easter a guy in my office brought in a giant shopping bag full of candy that his kid had collected at church, but had been forbidden to eat by his health-obsessed parents (and how messed up is that?). People converged on that thing like hyenas on a dead hiker. It was something to see. After the mushroom cloud of wrappers and saliva settled, the only thing left standing was a package of Peeps. Even the shopping bag was gone. The people in my office would eat the molding from around a set of storm windows if it was salty or sweet enough, but they draw the line at Peeps. The poor little yellow guys were still sitting there yesterday, over a week later.

— I don't really understand the obsession, but my brother's heavily into tracing our family history. He was having trouble finding info on a particular great, great, great grandfather (give or take a few greats), so he put the word out on the Internet. Somebody finally sent him a quote from a genealogy booklet the other day that said something along the lines of "Not much is known about him. He regularly attended meetings of Civil War veterans in Charleston, WV, and drank too much." Sounds about right. In a hundred years somebody will probably write the same thing about me, replacing the Civil War part with something about fast food hamburgers.

— Our kitchen sink was plugged up Monday, and we tried everything to avoid calling a plumber. We plunged, we snaked, we poured a plutonium-laced liquid, but nothing worked. We finally bit the bullet and had somebody come out yesterday. It was a relatively painless experience, but you never know that going in. During all this Toney found a website where people can pose plumbing questions, and a professional is supposed to post an answer. Here's one of the questions, which she e-mailed to me at work:

This is the second time weve been trough this! My Aunt has a beautiful home but because of her weight - she weighs 290 I'm 280, and my parents are both above 300lbs, we keep having to replace her fiberglass bathtubs. We tried putting in a castiron tub, but the weight, comibned with her's, resulted in the tub falling halve trough the floor and the livingroom ceiling below during the footboall game!!

She was lucky to be spared her life although she scrambled out of there and in her hurry fell out of the tub into the toiletbowl and cocked it sidways out' the floor. So's you can see we have a real mess here anyway we can reinforce the floor beneath so as to support a castiron bathtub?

Thank you for your kindly suggestions,

Phil280

— The summer concert season's getting ready to crank up here in Scranton, and they've got quite the lineup confirmed so far. Just a sampling: Poison, Warrant, Quiet Riot, Enuff Z'nuff, Styx, Bad Co., Billy Squier, Lynyrd Skynyrd, Deep Purple, Ted Nugent, Journey, Peter Frampton, John Waite…the list goes on and on. How exhilarating it is to be living in a place that's on the absolute cutting edge of popular culture!

May 1, 2001

— Those pains in the asses down at the health department have shut down my favorite local watering hole: John K's Pub! I'm stunned. How could this happen?! That place was an institution. Who cares if their kitchen was steeped in filth? If you're foolish enough to actually order food in a dump like that, you get what you deserve. No amount of government regulations can completely protect people from their own stupidity. Anyway, the squalor was a big part of the charm. Stinking busy-body bureaucrats, hell-bent on screwing around with anything that adds color to our bleak everyday lives... I drove by there Sunday, and the windows were covered in newspaper, as if the citizens need to be protected from even seeing inside, and two men were carrying out a large stainless steel cooler. I'm not ashamed to admit a single lager tear escaped one of my bloodshot eyes.

— Thanks to the new Who Wants to be a Millionaire? game, I found myself sitting in a booth at McDonald's yesterday afternoon mumbling to myself, "Benjamin Netanyahu? Yes, I think it's Benjamin Netanyahu", and then the former prime minister of Israel helped me score a free breakfast sandwich. I could not have predicted this event when I got out of bed yesterday.

— While the in-laws were driving cross-country, returning to America's Anus (Sparks, Nevada), they found a large bag of weed on the floor of a gas station bathroom. What to do? Should they hand it over to the authorities? Turn it in to the station's manager? Flush it down the toilet, so it doesn't end up in the wrong hands? Yes, those were all good options but...they smoked it.

— On a related note, I've been craving Chinese food for a few days, but this area doesn't have much to offer along those lines. The few places I've been brave enough to try serve up gloopy and sticky piles of crap shot through with shiny gray "meat." Damn, I'd kill for a half order of orange chicken from Frontier Wok in Burbank right about now. Anyway, I started

58

thinking about how a bunch of us at work used to go to a really good Chinese restaurant a couple days a week when we were in Atlanta. After we ordered our lunch combos by number (I always got #7 — cashew chicken), my boss would invariably say, "It doesn't matter which one you order, it's all gonna end up as #2 eventually." It was as inevitable as the sunrise.

May 4, 2001

— Hanging out in our backyard is a bird (or group of birds, who the hell knows?) that makes a sound almost exactly like our telephone ringing. Whenever the thing goes off, it triggers an instinctive reaction and I start the preliminary process of moving toward the phone. Then a split-second later I realize it's just that damned bird again, and I get really annoyed. I'm pretty sure it's mocking me (it's not like I can't hear the other birds laughing). One of these days I'm going to snap, and take to the yard in my draw's, screaming and waving a tennis racket — which will only confirm what the neighbors already suspect about me. If it's not one thing it's another. God, how I hate telephone birds.

— So, Tom Cruise is suing some guy who's going around LA claiming to be his homosexual lover? Big deal. I was called Jeff Gay almost daily when I was in junior high, and I never turned to litigation. But you know how hyper-sensitive some of those gay guys can be…especially the really short ones.

— There was a plastic card on my Wendy's tray yesterday that can be redeemed at a local clinic for a free cholesterol check. It seems a bit strange that a fast-food chain would be involved in something like this. It's like a donut shop offering no-cost ass measurements. Or a comic book store sponsoring a prom.

— I saw a truck today that had painted on its side: "Your scaffolding and bendable vinyl coil answers!" Talk about niche marketing.

— And finally, a rare transcript of life inside the bunker; this is an actual conversation that took place between me and my wife on Thursday morning:

Toney: You know what we should make this weekend?

Jeff: Wild passionate love?

Toney: No, deviled eggs.

May 7, 2001

— On Saturday Toney and I "celebrated" Cinco de Mayo by eating spinach quesadillas and nachos, and drinking lots and lots of margaritas. I know this may be shocking, and I probably shouldn't admit it, but we had no idea what we were celebrating. We just used it as a flimsy excuse to eat and drink to excess. It's the way we roll.

— As we celebrated foreign cultures by getting drunk in our family room, we also got sucked into a VH1 special about the 100 greatest rock 'n' roll moments on TV. It was pretty interesting, and had some good bits mixed in amongst the many cheap, calculated stunts by Madonna. I'd never seen Bob Dylan's television debut on the Johnny Cash show, for instance, and the Sex Pistols appearance on the British Today Show is always fun. But the thing that struck me the most were the commercials. I had no idea that vaginal dryness is such a problem in this country. We kept seeing ads for jugs of a clear liquid, made by the good folks at KY, that is apparently the answer to many a people's prayers. Toney said, over a salted margarita glass, "What are you supposed to do, stop in the middle of something and just slather it on?" Call me naive, but I wasn't aware that hordes of American women are apparently being driven by their devastating lack of personal moisture to purchase supplementary vaginal fluids over the counter. When I go back to work I need to make sure my retirement funds are positioned appropriately. I need to be on the forefront of this thing. In thirty years I'd like to point to our vacation home in Hilton Head, and be able to say, "A nation of bone-dry vaginas bought us that!"

— On Sunday I was walking in the park close to our house and some kid plowed into me on a bicycle. One zipped past at about 20 mph, then a second later another ran into the back of my legs, and brought my big ass down. We tumbled in a big pile, and when everything finally came to a stop he had a look of absolute terror on his face, like, "Oh shit, I've done it now." I was mildly irritated, but managed to laugh it off (despite the blood trickling down my left leg), and he seemed relieved. But in a sixth grade classroom, somewhere in Clarks Summit, PA, a kid will be telling a story about how he knocked down a fat man in the park, for days to come. Of that I'm certain.

May 17, 2001

— On Saturday we're going to Philadelphia to spend the day with Toney's cousin and aunt. Philly, of course, has a lot to offer. Independence Hall, the Liberty Bell, the Franklin Museum, South Street…the list goes on and on. But I'm fixated on one thing, and one thing only: a Chick-fil-A in every mall! I'm going to try to work it out so we have at least three meals there during the day. And I may take a cooler to haul back chicken salad. Only two days left, and counting…

— I watched the Behind the Music episode about Journey earlier in the week, and Steve Perry needs the shit kicked out of him.

— I mentioned that I'm going to be traveling to Greensboro, NC next month for a reunion of sorts with some folks I used to work with at a record store there. We've been e-mailing back and forth, working out the details and doing a little advance reminiscing. All this has caused me to recall a freak who used to come in the store when I was night manager. This guy would call us up and ask if we had a particular classical LP in stock, and if we didn't he'd keep going until he found one we did have.

Then he'd request that the album be put into a plastic shopping bag, and taped down real tight. Then a second bag should be taped on top of the first one. He wanted us to use a lot of Scotch tape, this seemed to be very important to him, and he wanted us to make sure it was an extremely tight little bundle when he got there to pick it up. Against my better judgment we would do this (we were a full service record store), and the guy would come in and stand there, rub the tape and lapse into a state of sexual euphoria. He'd stroke it lovingly, as his eyes glazed over and rolled back into his head. I've never seen anything like it. One of the other workers swore that the man had lengths of Scotch tape lining his forearms under his jacket. I shit you not.

May 21, 2001

— On Saturday we drove to Philadelphia to spend a few hours with Toney's cousin and aunt, and their family. It was fairly non-eventful, although before we met them we did browse around IKEA, and had Chick-fil-A for lunch. I'd wanted to have breakfast at Chick-fil-A as well, but we got a late start and screwed ourselves. Another missed opportunity. I cursed myself the rest of the day for not being more aggressive and pro-active in our pursuit of chicken and biscuits. This is no way to live a life. But the glass is half full; we managed to have lunch there, and it was damn good. Those fundamentalist Christians sure know how to cook up a chicken!

The Philadelphia annex of Toney's family are what you might call well-to-do. Her cousin lives in a neighborhood that undoubtedly includes surgeons and high-powered lawyers. The houses are large, the cars expensive, and the lands impressively 'scaped. They're all nice people, and unfortunately don't give me much ammunition for ridicule and mockery. I can't tell you how frustrating it is. The rest of Toney's family are like wildly-exaggerated sitcom characters, and these people are so normal and civilized. It's sad, really.

It was slim pickings, but there were a couple of minor highlights. At one point Toney's aunt went on at length about a pair of oven mitts she had bought, that are apparently the gold-standard of such items. She said you can wear them and pour boiling water over your hands, and not even feel it. I thought that was pretty amusing. I pictured her in her kitchen wearing her new mitts, with her hands plunged inside bubbling pots of water, her head thrown back in maniacal laughter.

Also Toney's cousin's in-laws came by, and they're very, very Italian. I believe they were actually born in Italy, but in any case they're the real deal. They brought a big bag of peas in the pod from their garden, and everyone started eating them raw and remarking about how "tender" they were. They were pretty good, I must admit, but I can't vouch for their tenderness, as compared to other raw peas I've had in the past. Somehow they got on the subject of their honeymoon, which took place in 1951. They had gone to a resort in upstate New York, near Niagara Falls, and Mickey Mantle and Billy Martin were there. They said the pair of Yankees stayed drunk the entire time they were there, drinking lots of beer and a green cocktail they're pretty sure is called a Grasshopper. Great story, except for the sissy mixed drink part. I don't want to think of The Mick with an umbrella in his glass, thank you very much.

All in all it was a pleasant day spent with sane people. Believe me, it hurts me more than it hurts you.

— On our drive home I became goofy with fatigue. I kept nodding off behind the wheel, and I was twitching like Andy Rooney. We pulled off the Turnpike to get out of the car for a few minutes, and to buy some caffeine. I was still loopy when I went in pursuit of giant Mountain Dews, and I somehow got turned around and managed to lose my wife and our vehicle — in the parking lot of a convenience store. Although I'm embarrassed to admit this, I went in one door and out another, and found myself completely baffled. Nothing was as it was before, and I momentarily panicked. Of course, Toney was watching all this from the car and laughing hysterically. It was like something off cartoons.

— Saturday night I had a few Yuenglings and watched Full Metal Jacket on DVD. I think I'm the only person in the world who had never seen it. Great flick, and now I can feel fully informed the next time somebody launches into, "Ahh, me so horny…I love you long time, Joe…fucky fucky…sucky sucky…" I'm a more well-rounded person today.

— Sunday morning I went out to mow the grass, and there was a neighbor a few doors down messing around in his yard as well. As I was filling the mower with gas in our driveway, a woman in a minivan drove up and stopped halfway between the neighbor and me. She rolled down her window and said, "I'll pray for you two this morning — IN CHURCH!" Shit lady, I know it's the Sabbath but doesn't all that Christian chicken count for anything?

June 1, 2001

— I'm about halfway through To Kill A Mockingbird again. It's the third time I've read it, and it still blows me away. An English teacher forced us to read it in high school, and it caused me to become a reader. Before that I mocked and threw stuff at people who read for pleasure. But this book made me see the light. Every page is an amazing achievement, and Harper Lee is a god. Who knows what would've happened if that teacher had made us read The Scarlet Letter, or some other pile of literary dullness? I can't help but think the quality of the enema humor you find here would've almost certainly suffered.

— Krispy Kreme is building one of their shiny silver temples of fried dough right down the street from where we live, easily accessible on my route to work. I swear, I'm gonna be one of those guys who has chest pains, and the fire department will have to cut the picture window out of our house to get me out. The world is conspiring against me: society has made my ass fat.

June 4, 2001

If weekdays zipped by like Saturdays and Sundays we'd be in good shape. It would be like living in Germany, without the scary language and the sausages. Don't they have fifteen-hour work weeks over there? Five hours a day, Tuesday through Thursday, then: beer, suspenders, & tubas! Shit, I thought they lost the war; why are we the ones who are working so hard? Maybe I'm a little confused on some of the details, but I'm not really talking about Germany here. I'm bitching about it being Monday morning again, so soon. How is it possible? It seems like Friday evening was yesterday morning. Or something.

And the stinking Germans sleep on…

June 12, 2001

— Speaking of dried up husks, I read that Bob Barker has signed a new contract to host The Price Is Right for another five years, which means he'll be doing a daily show at the age of 82. He's pushing his luck, in my opinion. It's only a matter of time before one of those big Samoans wins a car, picks Bob up and waves him around like a flag, then hurls him to the ground and causes his hip to explode like glass. It would be a sad sight indeed to see good ol' Bob Barker die onstage with his head wedged deep under "the Big Wheel," screaming, "I love you Betty White!!" I'd probably only be able to watch the bootleg tape twenty or thirty times.

— We went to the state park near our house with my parents over the weekend, and saw two women walking pet rabbits. They had the things outfitted with harnesses, and attached to dog leashes. I've seen a lot of things in my life, but never that. We stopped to pet them, and one went wild and started running around in frenzied circles. It was in the throes of some kind of bunny fit. One of the women had a big hunk missing from her forearm, and said the crazed one bit her earlier in the day. If that little bastard had bit me like that, I'd grab his leash and helicopter him above my head for about ten minutes and see if his attitude improved any.

— Before we left the park we stopped at the swimming pool concession stand for an ice cream cone, and I was once again amazed at the bizarreness of this world. When we walked up to the window we could hear loud opera music playing inside. The menu was impossibly cluttered, but we finally found what we were looking for. I ordered as planned, but Toney switched gears at the last second and said she wanted to try the cannoli. The hell?! Cannoli, at a swimming pool concession stand? As we waited we noticed they also have manicotti and tortellini and pierogies and other surprising items on the menu. After a while a man with a long white pointy beard stuck his head through the window and hollered, "Who ordered the canoli?" I sheepishly raised my hand, and he started telling me how he prepares it fresh everyday and it's all homemade including the cream - just like you'd get it in Italy. Then he told me not to go anywhere, and left and came back momentarily with a big tray of puff pastries (sfogliatelle, if you can believe it). "Aren't they beautiful?" he asked proudly. It was mind-boggling. We sat down at a picnic table, and Toney took a bite of her dessert and her eyes quickly rolled back in her head. "This is sooooooo good," she swooned. I took a bite, and it was indeed incredible. I went back for the puffs, and the guy chuckled and told me he knew I'd be back. One of these days real soon we're going to dinner there. That dude probably has a killer wine cellar under his hotdog stand.

— On Saturday our friends Steve and Myra stopped by for a quick visit. I've known Steve since something like second grade. When we were kids we were at each other's houses almost as much as we were at our own, and now we live in some far-flung place just 75 miles apart. Again, it's all so bizarre. On Sunday we were sitting in my living room drinking an ice-cold Yuengling, when Toney and my mother came home from shopping. Steve saw them drive up, began frantically chugging his beer, and ran to the kitchen and tossed his can in the trash. He didn't want my mom to see him drinking a beer. We're 38, and he has a master's degree for godsakes! It was like we were sixteen again, sneaking Miller High Lifes behind the bleachers at the high school. Hilarious. It's funny though, I don't think I'd have the stones to drink in front of his mother either. Some things are just burned into you, and there's no going back. Even now, Steve's mother could undoubtedly reduce me to tears within seconds. Sure I'm a man (kinda sorta), but there are limits to everything. It's like a fear of heights, or something primal. What can I say?

— On Sunday we took the folks out to some stores, and had lunch, and stuff like that. We were in a restaurant and saw a fat man with a ponytail applying a line of mayonnaise to each individual french fry before devouring it. I couldn't watch. Then I saw a fifteen or sixteen year old girl in a halter top with George Clooney's beard under each arm, and that didn't help anything either. Later we were in Old Navy and walked into a heart-stopping fart cloud that was causing a mini mosh pit to form in the middle of a retail store. My dad summed it up when he said, "Sshhew! That thing was still hot when we got to it."

God bless America.

June 15, 2001

You can tell a lot about a man by the way he conducts himself in front of a urinal.

A few months ago I mentioned the horrible infestation of consultants at my workplace. Even back then they were scurrying about everywhere, making creepy little nasally sounds, and generally throwing off the rhythm of everyone's working life with their all-knowing ways. Well, I'm sad to report that they've only multiplied and ratcheted up their smugness in the time that's passed. Maybe I'd be supremely pleased with myself too if I were fresh out of college, making eighty grand a year and contentedly sucking at the Corporate American Express teat, but I doubt it. I'm not a bastard.

I think it's their confidence that gets under my skin the most. They're too young to be so sure of themselves. When I was twenty-four I could barely put on a pair of pants by myself. These people burst into rooms, wearing their professionally pressed power ensembles, and begin emoting with gusto, just praying somebody will disagree with them about something. They live to set people straight.

Every fiber of my being tells me it's a charade, that they've been trained to play the part. It's all a house of cards, and every card is a Joker, in my highly biased opinion.

But it doesn't stop there; I don't like their voices either. Most of them talk through their noses, like they're from Chicago. But they're not from Chicago, they're from places like Dayton, Ohio, and that's simply not a good enough excuse. Also, they drive cars carefully chosen to telegraph both their high incomes and young ages, and they're geeky and pasty and go out running after work, not for health reasons but so they can tell people they go out running after work. They gush about their fancy expense-account meals in front of people who can't afford them, and they talk smoochy-smoochy love talk to their wives and husbands back home in Dayton or Glendale over company-subsidized long-distance lines for all to hear. Blaa! I just don't like them; they're squirrelly, and they're dangerous. And they have the power to wreck lives by justifying their professional existence. I've seen it happen.

Sometimes, in weak moments, I think I might be a little unfair about all this. I wonder if I'm simply jealous of their success. After all, didn't they work for what they've got? I'm not generally susceptible to class envy, I genuinely admire achievement, but I guess anything's possible. Or maybe it's their youth? I think that's a big part of it, to be quite honest. Not enough dues have been paid. They were probably playing wiffle ball five years ago, and now corporate hang on their every word. But if I don't see one of the vermin for a while, I start to build up some guilt. I feel a little ashamed of myself. What a common working-class clod I am!

Then I take a leak beside one of them, and all my suspicions are verified.

They explode into bathrooms like they own them. They start tossing greetings and salutations all around, as if they're running for elected office. After a few wink-wink nudge-nudge inside jokes, and possibly some good-natured back slaps, they saunter up to the porcelain and assume the position: chest out, feet apart, fists on hips. Think Superman deflecting bullets. Afterwards you can count on much vigorous, sustained shaking of the nozzle, as if there's so much there a little extra effort is called for, and then the part that really gets to me, a jaunty little snap! of their underwear waistband for punctuation. Urination punctuation.

It's that little dramatic flourish at the end that tells the tale. I'm king of the world! Even when I'm voiding my bladder, I'm superior to you. Hahaha!! Ka-slap! I am a master urinator! No one can touch my pissing! Hahaha!!

Slappety-ker-schlapp!!

A man who turns his bathroom habits into a performance piece is fundamentally flawed. I don't even think that's arguable. It's the height of arrogance.

But at least it gives me permission to hate them without that pesky guilt. That's the silver lining, I guess. And god, how I hate them.

— I'm getting ready to drive 500 miles to attend a reunion of some folks I used to work with at a record store in Greensboro, NC. It's been in the making for months, and I'm wondering if it can live up to the expectations. But I'm pretty excited. I haven't seen most of these people in ten or twelve years. We had a blast together in the old days, and it will be interesting to see if the magic is still there. I have a hunch it is.

Of course, you can read about it all right here, next week. I'll be back in the saddle on Monday.

Have a great weekend!

June 19, 2001

I once read that the human liver has the ability to repair itself, if given half a chance. I can't remember where I saw that, but all day Sunday I was clinging to it and needing for it to be true.

Saturday night was the much-anticipated Peaches reunion in Greensboro, NC. Peaches Records and Tapes was a big Tower-like record store where we all worked, more or less, from 1986 to 1989. Through some unlikely planetary alignment, we were a group of people who clicked, and actually seemed to like each other, brought together by fate and forced to wear matching denim smocks. I've had plenty of jobs, and almost without exception I've wanted to get far away from my asshole co-workers at the end of the day, but there was some kind of mojo working during the

Peaches years. We had fun on the job, and also hung out together after the workday was done. It was a beautiful thing, while it lasted.

A handful of us have stayed in contact over the years, mostly through e-mail, and a few months ago the idea of a reunion started getting kicked around. In the beginning I thought it was just talk, but to my surprise it came together with little difficulty. The list of people planning to attend kept getting longer and longer, and everyone seemed genuinely excited. The shit was actually going to happen! I was excited too.

And so, this past Friday I loaded up the Toyota and headed south. I picked out some CDs from the era for the trip, like the Smithereens, the BoDeans, Beastie Boys, Guns 'n' Roses, etc. etc. It took about nine hours to travel the 500 miles to my brother Tim's house in High Point, NC. I stayed with him and his wife Friday night.

We had dinner at a place I've always liked, called Ham's. The restaurant was packed, but the food was worth the wait. Then we hung out at their house and drank BEER and shot the shit for the rest of the night. Their friend Rain came by and joined in the festivities, and we stayed up until the middle of the night. At one point I went outside while Tim smoked a cigar on the porch, and I'd forgotten about the smothering humidity in the South. Holy shit. It felt like I had a blanket soaked in sea water over my head. I miss a lot of things about the South, but that's not one of them.

My brother cracked me up talking about somebody at his job who was written up for blatantly farting all over the place (or as Tim referred to it, "showboating"). Apparently this guy would just cut loose wherever the urge hit him, and some of the women complained when he blasted a couple their way while they were trying to eat a cheese sandwich in the break room. Some people can be so touchy. Tim told me that before The Man came down on him and ruined all his fun, this guy got a little overzealous and shit his pants a couple of times. And instead of toning down the theatrics, he just started carrying extra underwear with him. I've always admired a man who sticks to his convictions.

After a little sleep, a lot of coffee and a shower, I headed to Greensboro on Saturday afternoon. It'd been years since I'd been there, so I drove around a while. The first stop was the old Peaches building, and it was a pretty depressing sight. The store closed a year or so ago, but the signs are still up and the racks are still where they always were. The parking lot has grass growing up through the cracks, busted malt liquor bottles are everywhere, and a couple of old junked cars have been abandoned in front of the late, great record palace. A handmade sign is taped to the inside of one of the windows that reads, "This store is closed, and will not reopen." This is where it all began, and now it's like something out of Damnation Alley. What an absolute bummer.

I used to live in an apartment complex just a couple of blocks away, so I decided to swing by and see how it had fared during the last dozen or so years. Considering the condition of the store, I figured the apartments would be falling down or completely burned out. I was expecting a scene from The Bronx, circa 1981. But the old homestead looks good, at least as good as when I lived there. Very confusing.

I drove up High Point Road, the main drag through town, then around the college. No major changes. It felt strange being back, kinda dream-like. Brad, one of the ex-Peachsters, was supposed to page me around three o'clock to make plans for some pre-party partying, and at around four I decided to take matters into my own hands and went into the bar to begin the day's intake of BEER, and await his call. He works overnight, and sleeps during the day, so I didn't want to call him and maybe wake him up. Maybe he'd had a bad night or something. So I waited, and an aging hippie woman with a potbelly started talking to me about lawyers. She told me that if I ever needed one, I should seek out the dishonest variety. An honest lawyer doesn't get anything done, she said. Then she added that if she'd hired a dishonest lawyer, she'd be in Puerto Rico by now.

"Can I use your phone?" I asked the bartender. Brad was awake, but he'd misplaced my pager number. He came to the bar and I followed him back to his apartment. There we drank BEER, and talked until it was time to meet some other folks for dinner.

We ate at a cool little place called Wild Magnolia. It's a Cajun restaurant, in a building that was a Volkswagen garage when I lived there. We met ex-Peachsters David and his wife Michele, and Eugene and his fiancee Susan. What a great time! It was like the past dozen years never happened. We just picked up where we left off, and the ladies jumped right in as well. We had spicy food, in my case jambalaya, and a lot more BEER. It was a hell of a good time. The evening was getting off to a good start.

After the restaurant, we all went back to Brad's apartment for even more BEER and some continued conversation, until it was time to hit the bar for the main event. And this is where things start getting a little fuzzy on me. I think the five hours of drinking at this point was starting to take its toll. The rest of the evening happened really fast.

There was no reason to discuss where the reunion would take place, it would be at College Hill Sundries, of course. We'd logged many hours in the tiny BEER bar, and it was the only logical choice for such an event. As soon as we walked in I spotted Cambo, and his wife Lilana. We started talking, and Jeff came in, then Adrienne. Allyson was there, and so was Chuck. It was all so bizarre. It was like 1988 again, and everybody seemed completely comfortable with each other. If I hadn't been so drunk, I probably would've started crying at the simple beauty of it all.

Nobody puked, there were no fistfights, and the cops weren't called. It was just a bunch of friends hanging out in a bar. With the possible exception of myself, there wasn't a single asshole in the bunch. No tabloid behavior took place, but it was still remarkable. Of course, much more BEER was consumed during the evening — much more. By the time Jeff announced he was going to move on to a "gay bar, where they have air conditioning" I was surprised that many hours had passed. It felt like minutes. We stayed until they wouldn't let us stay anymore.

Outside on the sidewalk I mentioned that I needed a souvenir of the evening. Adrienne ripped down a band flier and handed it to me, but that wasn't going to do the trick. I tried to convince anyone who would listen to please remove the stain glass window from the bar, so I could take it home with me. Surprisingly, there was little enthusiasm for my plan, but Brad suddenly took off running and ripped down a giant canvas sign from the front of a nearby clothing boutique that said, OPEN. I had my souvenir.

I crashed on Brad's couch, and morning arrived almost as soon as my head hit the pillow. I didn't feel like moving, but I had a nine hour trip ahead of me. I knocked on Brad's bedroom door, and told him I was leaving. For some reason he didn't look like he felt too good. We said our goodbyes, and I started one of the longest days of my life.

Tired and sleepy, hungover or maybe still a little drunk, is no way to drive 500 miles. Add to that the inevitable worries that I had offended somebody, or made a fool out of myself the night before, and it translates into a miserable day. I stopped at a Waffle House for some food and coffee, but couldn't really eat. I remembered the first time I visited a Waffle House in Greensboro years ago. I told the waitress what I wanted, and she just pivoted on her heel 45 degrees, and hollered the same thing I had just said, to the cook. I thought hell, I could've done that. Then I made a mental note to someday open a chain of restaurants where people just come in, seat themselves, and scream their orders in the direction of the kitchen. ROAST BEEF! TATERS!!

I couldn't listen to music because it made me sleepy, so I kept surfing the radio dial for something other than church. I heard some weird crap traveling across Virginia: an American Top 40 show from 1986 (?!), a pointless radio drama about a couple of strangers who survived a plane crash, a talk show where people were calling in guessing who Gore and

Bush were going to choose as their running mates (??!!). The experts seemed to agree it would be John Kerry and Christine Todd Whitman. But the worst of the bunch was ESPN radio. Are there any more cliched people on earth than athletes? They all say the same thing in interviews: "Well, I just try to go out there every day and do the best job I can. Sometimes it works out for your side, and sometimes it doesn't, but that's the name of the game…" Zzzzzz.

After I got my second wind, somewhere in Maryland, I popped in the CD David had made to commemorate the previous evening. It had a lot of the stuff we listened to in the store, and it sounded great. My ugly-ass picture is on the back cover, and it made me laugh.

Twelve years is way too long.

June 26, 2001

— A really scary thought has been crossing my mind lately, I've been batting around the idea of buying a tent trailer. I'm thinking it might be a good way for Toney and me to see New England on the cheap, before we're transferred again to God knows where. I have visions of camping on the coast in Maine, drifting off to sleep with lobster butter all over our faces, lighthouses in the distance. In reality, of course, it would be more like Jeff bitching incessantly because he's got sand in his shoe. And goddamn this humidity. And what's the deal with all these big-ass bugs, that thing was the size of a Matchbox car?! I'm not the most outdoorsy person, I admit, but I like the idea of paying twelve bucks a night to stay in campgrounds, instead of hotel rates. Hell, we could do some traveling on twelve bucks a night! And in the abstract, I like the idea of staying in a place, instead of just viewing it from a window. But whenever I mention this idea to friends who know me, the unanimous and instant reaction is uproarious laughter, so I guess I should put a little more thought into it.

— A few days ago I received a mailing for my twentieth high school reunion. Twentieth! Shit. I'm not just dealing in cliches when I say I don't feel as old as I am. Maybe it's the preservatives in all the beer I've consumed, but I honestly don't feel 38. As freaky as it seems, I can actually remember when my parents went to their twentieth: they were older than dirt to me at the time. No, I don't feel as old as I really am, but intellectually I know the clock is ticking and I'd be lying if I said it doesn't bother me. So I was doubly distressed to read that the opening night (the traditional vomit-spewing, tits-out beer bust) is being held at an old fart bar/restaurant. I've never set foot in this place, but when I was a young-buck toll collector I would watch all the sad and awkwardly dressed people filing in every night, from the safety of my toll booth across the street, and shake my head at the seediness of it all. It seemed like a bunch of traveling salesmen, trolling for seasoned skank. Maybe I'm wrong, but that's the impression I got. Now, apparently, this is our collective speed. How utterly depressing. I guess I should just quit fighting it, and order some Sansabelt slacks out of Parade magazine, get a gold pinky ring and a red sports coat, and start drinking scotch.

— This is part of an email I received yesterday, from MsDeniseWight in California:

Jeff- I am surrounded by the "Vegan Mafia," as I manage at the fifth largest natural foods co op in the United States. Nothing that my customers do or say surprises me anymore. When I reacted in horror to your house guest story, it was solely because of their awful manners, and total lack of consideration towards you and your good lady wife. Here is a good natural foods store story... Let me preface the story by telling you that we have a very large herb and vitamin department, and a staff there that does nothing but answer customer questions. Sometimes people get mixed up and think that the staff of natural foods store clerks are doctors/nutritionists/shrinks. One fine day, a gentleman approached one of the staff, complaining of some sort digestive upset. To emphasize the point, he pulls out a baggie with one of his turds in it, and says something to the effect of "look at this and tell me what is wrong!" We had to ask him to leave and take his bag of shit with him....

I don't know which part is funnier: the fact that a guy was waving around a bag of his own crap in a grocery store, or that some people consult store clerks with their medical questions. These are the same people, I'm sure, who "just can't trust" doctors. Hilarious. Thanks for sharing the story.

Until next time…

June 29, 2001

A few very random things:

— I just about soiled my panties earlier in the week when my boss showed up at my office unannounced. Since I'm in Scranton and he's based in southern California, I don't see much of him. And on the rare occasion that he does visit, I'm certainly told in advance. But I was sitting at my desk Wednesday morning and heard his voice. I thought I was hallucinating, but there he was talking to the department secretary! I'm his only employee here, and a surprise visit could only mean one thing. Sweet mother of Jesus, I thought, this is it: balls are about to be separated from their host. My heart sank. I was going to be unemployed in Scranton, PA! How did I get to this point; who could've predicted it? Dear god, what would I do?! But apparently there was nothing to it. He had a meeting with some hotshot in another division, and business in NYC the following day. We talked for a couple of hours, he thanked me for my efforts, and was gone. Holy shit.

— Yesterday afternoon I looked at myself in a mirror at work and I had a large zit on the side of my nose. It was roughly the size of a Certs breath mint. Who knows how long I'd been walking around with that thing? How many conversations had it dominated, without my knowledge? (Thinking back, I did notice that people had been taking on a slightly hypnotized look when I spoke to them. I just thought I was a mesmerizing conversationalist.) I'm 38 years old, what's it all about? Zits?! I'm a mess.

— And finally, I'd like to share a funny note I received from a reader. It came from Chris, and it's in reaction to my recent mention that I was contemplating the purchase of a tent-trailer.

Hey-

Before you purchase any type of fold out camper/trailer/foldout/living quarters type thing, I thought I'd share this with ya.

Two years ago, before my father in law left his 27 year marriage to pursue sex again with his high school sweetheart and my mother in law pursued an abnormally large new set of tits, they went on a vacation out west. They took my wife's two younger sisters, 8 and 13 at the time, around the country with an above referenced device attached to the back of their car. After showing their young daughters the family fun of Bourbon Street and the safe environment of Houston, they proceeded to venture into the Arizona desert with their traveling apartment.

The wind caught hold of the flattened device and began to waver around behind their car, eventually flipping them over eleven times in the desert. Both my sister in laws got broken ribs, my mother in law got a bloody nose and my father in law got a good ass chewin' from my mother in law for buying such a stupid attachment to the car. The thing opened up and all their belonging for the trip scattered across the open horizon.

Suddenly, out of nowhere, an Indian appeared like a hallucination to Jim Morrison. He helped them gather their belongings, comforted my sister in laws, hit on my mother in law, and proceeded to tell my father in law what an idiot he was for buying such a stupid attachment to his car and putting his family's life at risk in the desert. The Indian then disappeared like a box of crackers in Bosnia.

My inlaw family had to rent a car, drive home and go their separate ways.

If they had only bought a van…..

Thanks, Chris! That's good stuff. I'd never considered that the trailer could act like a hang glider in wind storms, but now that you mention it… I can't seriously see myself dragging around one of those things, but it appeals to the cheap little bastard inside my head.

You guys and gals keep those cards and letters coming. The more you write, the less I have to.

Have a great weekend!

July 2, 2001

— Toney said we were going to have spaghetti for dinner on Friday, and I imagined big heat-generating pots of boiling water on the stove, and suggested we meet somewhere instead. After a complex and extended discussion, we decided on the Old Country Buffet (hey, there's not a lot to choose from...). It's one of those places where you pay one price, and can eat until you black out. A man of my size has, of course, been to plenty of buffet restaurants, but this one is fairly decent. Predictably, though, the whole experience turned out to be a fiasco. The place was completely packed with the hideous and the morbidly obese, and we had to stand in line as if we were about to board a thrill ride. I generally have a big problem with waiting in line for the privilege of giving away money, but I could smell food in there, so I made an exception. After we finally paid our boarding fee, we had to remain in a staging area for a mummified woman to show us to our seats. The place was crazy. I saw a man in silhouette sitting by the window folding a foot-long breaded cutlet into his mouth, and I noticed a woman gnawing on what appeared to be a meat apple. A man who probably took his driving test in a horse-drawn carriage smiled toothlessly at his handler through a beard of heavy gravy. There was activity everywhere, nobody remained in their seats for long, and the food bar area was like a mosh pit. The food itself was good enough, but it was such a hassle to get at it, there was no way in hell it could've been an enjoyable experience. It's bad enough to have to jockey for position in front of a vat of macaroni and cheese, but it's really hard to take when the people jumping in front of you are still chewing their previous yield. People are full-blown disgusting.

— Saturday afternoon we drove about a hundred miles to look at tent-trailers at an "RV Super-Center." It's a scary prospect, but I'm slowly becoming sold on these ridiculous contraptions. They look silly to be sure, but they're pretty cool. Most have two king-sized beds (tested at 1100 pounds!), and they're surprisingly spacious. You can get them with air conditioning (although the guy told us we probably wouldn't need it, living so close to the Poconos…), and some even have a bathroom and shower. I could never in a million years take a dump in a tent trailer, separated from the general population by only a thin layer of canvas, but they offer the option if you're up for that kind of thing. You can also buy a screened room that attaches to the front of the whole deal, and you've got yourself a portable apartment. And the best part is, they're relatively inexpensive. I still can't picture myself pulling a trailer down the interstate, but I have a feeling it's in my future. Who could've predicted such a thing?

July 5, 2001

Tuesday night we loaded some high-sodium snacks into the Toyota and headed to our borough's big fireworks extravaganza. It's held at the middle school, out in the country, and we'd never been before so we didn't really know what to expect. We'd heard that it's quite the shindig, and those rumors turned out to be true. There's a huge open field in front of the school, and a large pond. The place was already crawling with people when we got there, and it was still a long way from sunset. We walked around, taking in all the activity, and checking out the many concession stands hawking french fries, potato pancakes (?!), corndogs, etc. etc. There were several of those big inflatable deals, where kids are offered the opportunity to climb inside a shelter and jump up and down for pleasure. Neon glowsticks were everywhere, for whatever unfathomable reason.

It was a fun evening. The setting reminded me of old photographs I've seen of town picnics in the early 1900's, except there were far fewer top hats. People had lawn chairs and blankets, there was lots of food and laughter, and a general vibe of friendliness and warmth hung in the air. It was a wholesome good time, the positive side of small-town living.

But it wasn't a complete Surf Report washout. I did see a group of teenage boys smoking dope in the woods, and quite a few teenage girls who obviously resented society's insistence on the wearing of clothes. And I saw a man so ugly I think I actually recoiled. He was wearing a cracked and faded Kenny Stabler football jersey. Yes, Kenny Stabler. And his head was simply unfortunate. He'd apparently been born without the luxury of a chin. His face began sinking back towards his neck just below the nose, so his ruby-red lips were at an approximate 45-degree angle when he was looking straight ahead. It had kind of a funnel-shape, if you can imagine a funnel with a fat spout. And his hair was sort of a modified Michael Landon, and was dyed jet-black with a part so wide you could drive a Matchbox car through it. I couldn't stop looking at him; he was the complete package — something to be savored. I cursed myself for not bringing a camera. And we also observed a group of obese people passing Frisbee at such close-range they were basically just handing it to each other. Dammit, the camcorder would've come in handy too. Next year.

But all in all, it was a good time. We didn't come fully prepared, but we had a blanket in the car so we spread it out on the grass beside the pond. I was horrified to see that it had a huge brown stain in the middle. Toney said it was coffee, and nothing to be ashamed of, but I positioned myself awkwardly in an attempt to hide it. People probably thought I had the palsy. But we laid there and listened to the hot sounds of Exact Change, and their medley of terrible singles of the recent past. And finally it was time for the main event.

It was supposedly "choreographed", but as far as I could tell they just played random songs in the background. There was no apparent relationship between the music and the fireworks. Of course, as soon as it started I began imagining all the horrible things that could go wrong. I was weary of fiery embers falling from the sky and going down the back of my shirt. I was watching for the flaming arm of a worker to be launched into the sky, as a result of a quick fuse. And I imagined one of the tubes tipping over, and a large "entertainment explosive" lodging in the small of my back as I ran screaming like a girl. None of this stuff happened, however, and a splendid time was had by all.

It was nice. We were genuinely happy as we sat in the holiday traffic jam, with our aching bladders and traditional wet asses. It made me want to rush out and paint stars and stripes on a curb somewhere.

Coming up next: According to Toney, Jeff will be attending a "luau" against his will on Saturday. This oughta be good. Stay tuned.

July 6, 2001

— Why are there no British baseball players? Don't they play cricket over there, or some shit? What's the problem?

— My old local watering-hole, John K's Pub, has apparently been de-maggoted and is about to rise from the health-department ashes as the State Street Bar and Grill. I've been watching from a distance as they've carted out loads of crap, and carried in lots of new crap. I don't know what to expect, but I'll be there to pass judgment once they open their doors. I'm a harsh critic, so it better be good. For instance, they better serve beer.

July 9, 2001

— On Saturday Toney dragged me to a "luau" at somebody's house I'd never really met before, and we hobnobbed with dozens of complete strangers for several hours. Being a man with little to no social skills, it's the type of situation I normally go to great lengths to avoid. But it turned out to be relatively painless. I didn't really know what to expect from such an event; I had visions of a pig rotating in a giant pit in the backyard, torches and grass skirts, perhaps a little knife juggling. But they just hung up a sign that said "Luau!!", and yelled aloha whenever somebody came through the front door — instant island paradise, right here in Scranton. I suppose if they'd hung a sign that said "Kidney Dialysis!!" their kitchen would've been transformed into an outpatient clinic.

They may have called it something else, but it was just a normal everyday cookout, and nearly all of the people there were friendly. The host had a mild case of BO, but he's European, so make of that what you will. And he was wearing a pair of shorts that I would've strongly advised against, had he asked for my opinion. It benefits no one to see anything that high up a man's disgusting, hairy thigh. Good god man, cover it up! There was a barrel of Yuengling lagers on ice out on the deck, and incredible amounts of meat. Mr. Stinky kept grilling and grilling and grilling, supply far outstripping demand, until there was a sizable mound of glistening meats weighing down the dining room table. People would just walk past and poke their forks at the mound without even stopping, and come away with hotdogs, or hamburgers, or ribs, or steaks. It was something to see.

Just beyond the backyard was thick woods, and at one point the brush began to shake, then there was a parting, and a woman emerged brandishing a relish tray. I rubbed my eyes to make sure I wasn't seeing things, but it was true. She almost floated across the yard, sat the tray down, and disappeared back into the woods without saying a word. It was spooky. It was like some raw produce Field of Dreams. The Celery Field of Dreams. I was tempted, but I never got up enough nerve to eat any of the items on that plate. There might've been magic in those baby carrots. Or poison. I stayed away.

The music selection was very interesting as well. Very exotic, and very tropical. I believe it was the Cocktail soundtrack, on an endless loop. I know I heard that irritating "Kokomo" song by the Beach Boys roughly 85 times. At one point I took a seat in the dining room, with the mound positioned between me and the stereo, attempting to block out the offending sounds with a meat shield. It actually worked pretty well. Not even Mike Love's nasal drone could penetrate that powerful wall of cutlets. I recommend this technique highly, if you ever find yourself in a similar situation. Cooked meat makes an excellent sound buffer.

Yes, after all the dread, it didn't turn out half bad. Even though nearly all of my conversations went this way, it could've been far worse:

Other guy: Nice day, isn't it?

Me: Yep, sure is.

Other guy: I thought we might get some rain this morning, but it turned out to be really nice.

Me: Yeah, I'm just glad that humidity finally went away.

Other guy: Me too…

Me: …

Other guy: …

Me: Need another beer?

Other guy: You read my mind!

July 12, 2001

— Number 4376 in a series of things that irritate the hell out of me: When you pre-pay for gasoline, the last ten cents takes as long to pump as the first $9.90. Why does it have to slow down that much? I almost always lose my shit and end up yelling at the pump like an escaped lunatic.

— Toney's been buying a lot of exotic mustards lately, and I can't handle them very well. Australian mustard, white wine mustard, mustard that looks like fresh-cut baby shit… What's wrong with the 49-cent bottle of French's with the nozzle on top? You know, the kind that requires you to dispose of that little plug of crusty grossness, then let the pre-cum yellow water run out before use? That's the real deal. I'm not a big fan of novelty condiments.

July 16, 2001

After work on Friday I stopped at a grocery store to buy buns and a half-pound of cole slaw. While surfing the 'net on company time I'd developed a powerful hankering for "West Virginia hotdogs", and that required finely chopped cole slaw. Through my travels I've learned that slaw is not a common hotdog topping, except in The Mountain State. I can remember being in Florida as a kid, and seeing signs that said "West Virginia style hotdogs." We couldn't figure out what they were getting at. Our first suspicion was that it was some kind of yukkety-yuk hillbilly joke — West Virginians have been conditioned to always be on the defensive. But we finally stopped to ask, and "We put cole slaw on 'em," was the answer. We just looked at each other, cartoon question marks levitating above our heads. Doesn't everybody put cole slaw on 'em? It was bizarre to think that people wouldn't put cole slaw on 'em. And we're the ones who are out of step?

I've never stopped eating them that way — I just have to build them myself now. And they're damn good. Here's how you do it: put hotdogs on buns and wrap everything up in paper towels. Stick it in the microwave for about twenty-five seconds per dog, then pile high with quality cole slaw and nothing else. It has to be finely chopped, it can't be that stringy shit with the fancy-pants purple cabbage and all that garbage. KFC makes perfect hotdog-toppin' slaw if you can't find it anywhere else. Yum. It's as good as anything you can buy at Ruth's Chris Steakhouse, and it costs pennies. And don't worry, modern science has developed amazing ways to get your heart re-started once it's seized up.

But I'm getting way off the subject. Through experience I know that a particular deli in a particular grocery store offers the perfect grade of slaw required for my little project, so I went out of my way to go there. Sometimes this place is a madhouse, so I was pleased to see there was only one other person at the counter when I walked up. She was eating licorice, right off the shelf, which instantly annoyed me. It disgusts me to see people walking around grocery stores eating the merchandise, and then running the wrapper through the checkout line. Pigs. But she was getting turkey or something, and she'd be gone soon. Or so I thought.

After the turkey, she ordered something else. Then something else. The woman behind the counter kept saying, "Will that be all?" and the answer kept being no. The licorice-eater was around forty, and bursting out of clothes designed for teenagers, and was casually pacing the length of the glass cases and asking questions about various items within. "How's the potato salad?"…chomp, chomp, chomp… "What different kinds of ham do you have?" …smack, smack, smack… "Can I have a sample of the Italian salad?" My blood pressure was slowly rising with each nasally question, and it didn't help that she had a severe New York accent. I have my own set of prejudices, thank you very much.

It just kept getting worse and worse. She started asking for an eighth-pound of stuff. An eighth-pound! And she wouldn't let the woman off if it went over to say, one-seventh. She insisted on exactly one-eighth of a pound. And she had a condescending attitude toward the worker that really baked my beans. Then she ordered one slice of meat loaf — yes, one slice — and waited until the poor lady had wrapped it up, then added, "Oh, I wanted a little gravy on that too." It would've been justifiable homicide at that point. If I had been behind that counter I would've flicked a spoonful of gravy in her fat face. "There ya go, bitch."

I simply couldn't believe what was going on before me. This disgusting sow had complete disregard for everyone else around her. You could tell she firmly believed she was the only thing that mattered, and everyone else was just going to have to wait until she had completed her casual shopping trip. It was her time. By god, she had a right. I am obnoxious cow, hear me roar!

By this time a line had built up behind me, and the woman under siege called for backup. A young kid appeared and asked what he could get me, and I told him a half-pound of cole slaw. He flopped it onto the scale and it was .63 pound, and he asked if it was OK. I practically shouted, "Yes, that's fine! Close is OK for me! I don't have a problem if it's not exactly perfect! And, yes that's all I need today! I'll get out of the way so you can help some of these other good folks!" I was expecting applause, but there was none. Everybody just looked at me, and blinked with confusion. Yes, I was the crazy one.

Cole slaw on hotdogs isn't the only thing I miss about West Virginia.

July 19, 2001

— This past weekend I needed a haircut, so I went by the cigar store to see if my favorite barber was available, and he wasn't. Again. The man apparently just works whenever he feels like it, and that ain't often. So I had a dilemma: either go back to the irritating "family" joint, or give the other barber in town one more chance — even though he pissed me off last time and I left in a huff. I started weighing my options, and finally decided to give the bitter barber another shot. Maybe he was just having a bad hair day last time.

When I was there before, the place was completely packed. There were more people waiting than there were chairs to wait in. But on Saturday Mr. Charming was all alone. It was late in the day, and he was perched in one of his barber chairs reading the paper. When I walked in he looked up and said nothing. He had a look of distaste on his face, like he'd seen me cross the street and had been praying to God I wouldn't come into his shop.

"Hi. Too late for a haircut?" I said.

"Just passing through town?" he replied.

What the hell did that mean?

"No, I live right around the corner."

"What street?"

I told him.

"Have a seat," he said.

I felt like I'd just won the fastest-finger contest and had earned a place on stage with Regis. Or the anti-Regis.

After we'd established what type of sheering I desired, he asked who had cut my hair in the past, and I foolishly mentioned the "family" place. "Fuckin' beauty parlor," was his bitter reply. I don't think I'd ever caused a barber to use the word "fuck" in my presence before. One step forward, two steps back. He went on to grill me about the kind of work I do ("DVDs…is that those circles?"), repeatedly asked if we had a theft problem on account of all the Mexicans (?!), railed against the current state of labor in the country ("We've become a service nation, we don't build anything anymore"), immigration laws, NAFTA ("Four dollars an hour will buy a lot of tacos"), and various other little things. When he found out I'd moved here from California he practically recoiled in horror. "Oh, I couldn't live in that place," he said without elaboration. Then before I left, he asked again about all the Mexicans at my workplace, and their rampant thievery. When I told him I wasn't aware of a problem, he looked disappointed. Heck, I'm not even aware of any Mexicans, I thought.

He built me a damn good haircut though.

— In any office I've ever worked there's been at least one person (almost always a woman) who is constantly sick with ailments the doctors can't diagnose, and who enjoys nothing more than discussing the endless medical procedures at length. My current office is no different. The department secretary has been to a half-dozen doctors since I've been here, and none of them can help her. She's fatigued, gets hives, and continues to put on weight even though she doesn't eat much (hahahaha!). She also suspects that her immune system has shut down. Whatever. I've become an expert at tuning most of it out. But my ears perked up earlier in the week when I overheard her telling someone she had an appointment on Tuesday to see a faith healer. Suddenly I became deeply concerned with her plight, and needed details.

Supposedly this "healer" came down with inoperable cancer a few years ago, and was visited by an angel who cured her of the disease in exchange for adopting the power to heal, and a promise to help the sick during her extended stay on Earth. I'm not clear on whether the angel set the $125 per session fee, or if that was arrived at later.

This woman spends most of her time in Germany, where she helps some of the greatest medical minds of our time diagnose diseases, but once a month she returns to Scranton to help stamp out hometown sickness. In fact, she recently cured my co-worker's aunt's arthritis, and she was at the Fourth of July picnic without her crutches. Most of the family had never seen Edna walk without them!

Yesterday I practically leapt at her when she came through the door. "How did it go?!" I demanded. I think she was starting to get a little suspicious of my sudden compassion, but she still couldn't pass up the opportunity to talk about it.

The woman never performed a formal examination, she just sat across a desk from her and talked and put strange oils on her hands (to improve reception?!). Then she proclaimed that her patient had an infection of the nervous system, and the infection must be removed. She said that a conventional doctor would never be able to diagnose her true problem, that they'd simply pump her full of steroids and send her on her way. Luckily she'd come to the right place though.

At one point the "doctor's" stomach growled and she yelled inexplicably, "See!?!"

She had the patient lean across the back of a chair, and she moved her hands up and down her back an inch or so from her skin. She began chattering and talking nonsense, occasionally clapping her hands and snapping her fingers. Her eyes were also rolling back in her head, she was gurgling and her mouth was hanging open. I nearly swallowed my tongue trying not to laugh. She said she could feel her skin heat up wherever her hand passed, and could sense that something was going on inside her body.

After the "procedure" the "doctor" told her she was only able to remove 75% of the infection, because it was so advanced. It would take several more sessions to make her completely better. She also warned her patient that she would most likely feel flu symptoms for a few days, because her body had undergone the equivalent of major surgery. They set up an appointment to try to remove that pesky 25% of the infection that remained, for right after her next German-curing tour.

More to come…as Drudge would say, DEVELOPING HOT…

July 23, 2001

— Saturday night I got sucked into watching a bunch of "Pop-Up Brady" episodes. It's on Nick At Nite, and it's complete Brady Bunch shows, given the Pop-Up Video treatment. It's pretty fun. Like when they open the sliding glass door, a little bubble points out that there's "No glass." And during the Johnny Bravo episode the reason for the actors' sweat stains is explained. Also there was one scene where Mr. Brady grabs a basketball and shoots a basket out on the driveway, and the bubble reads, "Swish." Wonder what that means? Check it out, if you get the chance. It's time well spent.

— Sunday afternoon we went swimming with the couple who threw the big luau a couple of weeks ago. They're nice people, but he's Eastern European and has some hygiene issues. He's known around town as Stinky Ukraine. Well, I call him that anyway. On Sunday he was putting off a pretty powerful musk when we got there, and it only got worse as the day wore on. I kept asking him if he was going to go in the water, in hopes that the chlorine and other chemicals might neutralize some of the funk, but he said he'd rather sit in the sun and listen to the Yankees game. I noticed that people started moving their blankets and lawn chairs to other parts of the lawn. After about a half-hour we had a big section of grass all to ourselves. I couldn't stop worrying that they all thought I was the culprit. I can't imagine how it must be in Czechoslovakia on a hot August day. Forget the Kyoto Treaty, the UN should start airlifting in pallets of Sure. Holy crap!

I nearly tripped getting into the pool at one point, and had to windmill my arms like a cartoon character to keep from falling on a couple of terrified children below. "Mommy, a fat man almost fell on me!" After I got my footing, I looked up and about twenty people were laughing, including my own wife. I am a dork.

I also saw a sixty-or-so year old woman standing in the pool smoking. Can you believe that?! One of the lifeguards made her put it out, but she had it dangling off her lips out there for a good long time. That's a new one on me…and I'm from West Virginia. And I saw something that resembled a 400 lb. mound of pasty flesh with Randy Newman's head sitting on top of it, just standing in knee-deep water for what seemed like an hour. He barely moved. I think there might've been some brain-damage issues at play there. And I've said it before, but it's still true: the day I moved from LA to Scranton, I suddenly transformed into JFK Jr. Walking around this town I feel beautiful for the first time in my life. The chamber of commerce needs to capitalize on this fact. "You won't feel ugly in Scranton!" There's one for the coffee mugs and bumper stickers.

July 27, 2001

— The drought is over. I took a vacation day on Wednesday, so Tuesday evening I went to the beer store. In Pennsylvania you can't buy beer in a grocery store or a convenience store, you have to go to a beer store. And you can't buy anything smaller than a case, which is fine by me, but apparently causes some concern among the casual drinkers. Boo hoo for them, I say. If you can't run with the big dogs, then stay out of the soup kitchen. Or whatever. Anyway, I carried my beautiful, shiny box of Yuengling to the counter, and as the guy was ringing it up I asked him what was their best seller. To my surprise, he said, "You're holding it…That's it, by far" Yuengling lager?! I knew it was popular, but how could it be the most popular? How could a regional brand compete with the likes of Coors Light and Budweiser and the national mega-brewers? I mean, I've been to the Yuengling brewery, and it's extremely small; less than a hundred people work there. But they're apparently kicking Anheuser-Busch's ass - in northeastern Pennsylvania anyway. I rag on this place a lot, but they sure have better taste in beer than anywhere else I've lived. Yuengling lager is a great regional brew, and these people are passionate about it up here. That says something. I'm not sure what, but something. I'm sorry, but I'm getting a little emotional…

— I saw some women in dresses in Wendy's on my day off. They were in their early 20's, and obviously members of some kind of back-to-basics religious group (Amish? Quakers? Who the hell knows?), and had apparently never been to a fast food restaurant before. They stared at the menu board for an extended amount of time, with the intensity of a gambler watching a horse race. They seemed slightly frightened by the bright lights, and were generally ill at ease with the whole experience. Finally they summoned up enough courage to approach the counter, and placed their orders. Each paid from tightly clutched change purses, and seemed relieved once they'd made it through the ordeal. It was very entertaining to watch.

— My brother called a few nights ago and left a very serious-sounding message on our answering machine about one of our cousins. Apparently he was going in for an invasive heart test, because of recurring chest pains. From the tone of the message, it sounded pretty grim. I called him back the next day to see how it had gone, and my cousin was sitting right there in the living room with him. Oh, he's fine, he said. They didn't find any blockage or anything. We're getting ready to go to IHOP. It took a second for my brain to process what I had just heard. Heart patient…chest pains…hushed tones…emergency medical procedures…International House of Pancakes …sausages…white gravy… I'm not sure why I was surprised.

July 30, 2001

— Toney's cousin came to visit on Saturday from Philadelphia. One of her neighbors had to travel to Scranton to see a client, so she tagged along and spent a couple of hours at our house shooting the shit. The neighbor is a lawyer, and he had to meet with a client up here. The client was supposedly a guest at a church that was in the final stages of being built. Sometime during the evening he came out of a bathroom, tripped over some construction materials and fell into an empty baptismal pool, exploding his back. I laughed for ten minutes.

— We went to Don Pablo's yesterday afternoon, and I don't know if my standards are plummeting, due to lack of exposure, but it was damn good. Last time I was there I felt the food was bland, and probably prepared by a couple of white people from Binghamton, NY. That was just a few months after I'd moved here from LA. And yesterday, many months later, was like an orgy of Mexican delight. I felt like I was in Tijuana. I'm obviously slipping. Next I'll start thinking of places like Olive Garden and Panda Express as being exotic, like when I was eighteen. But we ate until we could barely walk, and drank frozen margaritas from comically oversized glasses. It was a good time, even if it was just a lousy chain restaurant.

August 6, 2001

— Saturday morning I called my parents, as I do every Saturday morning, and when my Mom answered I could hear people talking and laughing in the background. "What's going on there?" I said, "it sounds like a barroom." She was in the middle of telling me that a couple of their old friends were in from North Carolina and had been staying with them, when I heard: "Is that Jeff, the gay boy?" — followed by uproarious laughter. (And one of the lead laughers, I'm almost sure, was MY DAD!) Gay boy? The hell?! "Are ya'll drunk?!" I asked. After she repeated what I said, the room again erupted in laughter. Shit. I was just calling to fulfill my weekly obligation; I wasn't expecting a flashback to Junior High gym class. I was a little shaken, and told her I'd call them back later, when they weren't so busy. She said, "OK," and hung up. And as she was putting the phone down, an avalanche of fresh laughter came buzzing out of my receiver. Sheesh.

— I took a fiction writing class in California, from a successful novelist who I came to respect a great deal. He's an ex-lawyer that gave up the big paydays to become a writer, and after a few lean years is actually supporting himself by writing fiction. I don't think most people realize how rare a feat that is. Anyway, one of the things he discussed, that has stuck with me, is his appreciation for Dean Koontz. I was a little surprised, because I'm pretty much a snob when it comes to books and music. A writer as successful as Koontz just has to be a hack, in my way of thinking. Product cranked out for the masses, the literary equivalent of Cheez-Wiz, right? Well, not according to this guy. He said Koontz wasn't born with overwhelming natural talent, but has turned himself into an almost great writer through hard work and sheer determination. He views him as a great inspiration to all aspiring writers — proof that you don't need to be an F. Scott Fitzgerald to become an accomplished author. I'm a little skeptical, but I'm going to read a couple of his books. I've already been laughed at during a phone conversation with my parents, had my romantic visions of small town America booted around, and been robbed of my ability to help jump-start the economy. What's a little more disillusionment in the grand scheme of things?

— I received a really funny note from a loyal Surf Reporter a few days ago, and he's given me the OK to share it with you folks. We both suspect that the statute of limitation has probably run out by now. It's from Chris, and he's telling me about some of the reasons he left West Virginia, years ago. Here are a few excerpts:

Yeah, the apartment was in Spring Hill, but it was over somebody else's apartment. I got evicted after I bought a waterbed and the weight of it crashed through the floor into the apartment downstairs. I was paying for that until I left the state. Still owed $4000 in damages. That's right. I AM a fugitive from justice. Never left a forwarding address. I'm sure the old woman I rented from is dead now. But that's another story.

Obviously, I wasn't going to let that go without a follow-up, so I wrote him and asked for some additional information…

It actually landed in the bedroom of the couple below. Luckily, it happened in the mid afternoon, so no one was home. They were good friends of mine, so they didn't even bother with asking me to replace their lamps, bed, and womanly trinkets all over their destroyed dresser. The floor (mine) and the ceiling (theirs) looked like a hurricane had gone through. Their carpet was also saturated. They had renter's insurance and everything was covered, as far as their shit. I paid about 700 dollars on the reconstruction and skipped the state. The landlady's name was Icie Bear (no shit). She never knew I moved the waterbed in, and didn't realize I was using her water spigot to fill it up. I turned it on and it was taking forever. I just went to work and left it on. When I got home, the mattress was 5 feet tall. I think this may have weakened the floor. I siphoned the water out to the appropriate level and turned on the heater. Got the best night's sleep I had in months. I was anxious to try it out with my girlfriend the next day. Went to her house to pick her up and when I got back the fire department was there. I owned a waterbed for one day. Didn't pay the payments on it either. No wonder my credit report is so screwed.

Thanks Chris, that's good stuff. If the estate of Icie Bear comes knocking, I promise to get up on my high-horse and refuse to reveal my sources on the grounds of journalistic privilege. I'll turn them away with volume and a tone of moral indignation. Don't worry, it works every time.

And that's it for this edition. Until next time…Gay Boy, over and out.

August 9, 2001

— It's so hot I'm losing the will to live. It's hot and it's humid, and it doesn't even cool down at night. Our house doesn't have air conditioning (don't get me started!), and when I get out of bed at 5 am it's freaking hot. When I get home from work: hot. Watching a little TV with my wife at night: goddamn hot. There's no escape. The temperature's the same outside as it is inside. There's no breeze. A demoralizing haze hangs in the air. We're using box fans that are so white trash they make me want to cry. I'm sweating like a sow. I'm in hell!

— I've been seeing an endless parade of so-called "weather experts" on cable TV droning on about the heat, and they all seem to agree it just feels unusually hot because it's been a mild summer so far. We're just not accustomed to it, they say. So, you see, it's partly our fault. We have to share some of the blame here, because we haven't adequately adapted to the heat. Bullshit. It's hot. Kiss my ass.

— We went to the mall a couple of nights ago, because they have air conditioning, and I saw a woman there with a four foot back. That is to say, her back was roughly four feet across at its widest point. I've never seen anything quite like it. We were walking past Old Navy and I couldn't figure out why they had curtains hanging in just one section of their front windows, and they suddenly stood up and walked away! It wasn't curtains at all, it was The Woman With The Four-Foot Back! When she sat down on one of the benches at the front of the store, and leaned against the glass, her impossible wideness filled one entire pane of glass. She wasn't even fat really, just extremely beefy — like she'd grown up baling hay in Russia. I got so excited trying to point her out to Toney, I bumped into someone and nearly knocked them to the ground.

I've got lots more to write about, but can't concentrate. I'll catch up next time. I'm going to go have myself a good cry…

August 13, 2001

— I know this will probably sound made up, but I swear it's true. Over the weekend I stepped up on the bathroom scales, and the little wheel whirled so fast and for so long I think I saw sparks inside the little window, and it finally stopped at 230. I stepped down and began yelling in protest, and the button on my shorts shot off and went behind the toilet.

— But did I take a rocketing pants button as a sign to get my shit together? Of course not. Sunday afternoon I went to the grocery store with the specific intention of buying Ruffles potato chips (the saltiest potato chip, and therefore the best) and a tub of some really good locally-produced dip called Helluva Good (I'm not lying). When I pulled onto the lot I saw a sign that said, "Chicken Barbecue Today." I got really excited, because once a year this store holds a "customer appreciation day" and sets up several gigantic grills in the parking lot, and cooks hundreds and hundreds of chickens. Then they sell complete dinners for 99 cents each. And they're really good; people buy them by the dozens. When I opened the door of my truck, the smoky smell of cooking poultry rushed in and I became powerless. I went inside the store, bought the chips and dip, then walked over and bought two chicken dinners. Then I went home and ate until I couldn't eat anymore. Then we had dinner.

— Speaking of eating, I was in Wendy's Saturday afternoon and a big group of teenagers came in. I'd say they were about fourteen or fifteen, and there was roughly the same number of boys and girls. I sat and observed as I ate my #1 combo with cheese, careful not to stare. I didn't want people to think they had to rush out and consult the Megan's Law CD-Rom, or anything creepy like that; I just like to watch people. But I saw some things that made me feel really uneasy, things that I knew but had forgotten or blocked out: another one of God's cruel jokes. The girls were cute and mature and confident and restrained…and the boys were tall and awkward and zitty and way too driven to impress. It was a sad display, and I felt the pain of my horribly ill-equipped brothers. I wanted to pull them aside and reassure them that the zits will one day go away, and they will soon discover the confidence-boosting magic of distilled spirits. But, of course, I'd never do something like that. They've got to find their own way, as I did. Besides, I don't care that much. Screw 'em.

— Toney and I watched several episodes of a show called Trading Spaces Saturday night, over a few bottles of Yuengling. She'd told me about it many times, and she wanted me to check it out during a "marathon" they ran that day, on some esoteric cable channel (TLC? Who the hell knows?). The basic deal is, they find two neighbors who agree to allow each other to redesign and redecorate a single room in each other's home. The show gives them a thousand dollar budget, and provides each with the services of a professional interior designer. I have to say, it was great entertainment. The designers are mostly artsy and pretentious, and have really bizarre ideas ("I'm thinking that maybe we could completely cover this wall in moss."). And the homeowners are generally suburbanites with pretty conservative tastes. There's a lot of friction between the designers and the neighbors ("Bill's going to absolutely kill us for doing this to his house!"), and a lot of suspense builds up as you wait to see how it'll turn out, and especially what the owners will think of it in the end. Maybe it was the beer, but I got completely hooked and continued to watch even after Toney had gone to bed.

August 16, 2001

— We're going to West Virginia on Sunday, and will be there most of next week. That means no updates to the site after Saturday, until the following weekend. Yes, that's right…you won't know what television shows I'm watching or what the weather's like or what I had for dinner (or the amount of flatulence it generated). It'll be a loss I know, but please be strong.

— Speaking of my old stomping grounds, I've been following an odd story through the Drudge Report (yeah I read Drudge, what of it?) about a "top secret" cloning operation in the "rural hills" of West Virginia. Supposedly a French doctor has set up shop in an abandoned high school there, and is working feverishly to clone a 10-month old baby that died in 1999. He's reportedly being funded by a wealthy WV lawyer, who is the father of the baby. The articles read like something from the Weekly World News, but they're apparently reprints from a British newspaper (?!). It's all so bizarre and, frankly, unbelievable. The town where this is supposedly going down is less than ten miles from where I grew up! I asked my parents, who still live in the state, if they'd heard anything about it. But instead of a real answer I got a "there he goes again" chuckle. They think I'm making it up. No respect. Anyway, I'm planning to check it out for myself when I'm there next week. Hopefully I won't be shot in the back by a UFO cultist wearing an aluminum foil hat.

— There are many interesting things about the WV cloning story, but I especially like the depiction of the city of Nitro as being in the "rural hills." Any story about the state, produced by outsiders, invariably depicts it as nothing but hollers and moonshine stills and Hatfields and McCoys and barefoot hicks living in shacks with their bloodhounds. Also, there's an apparent FCC requirement for TV networks to have banjo music playing in the background whenever a feature story is done about the place. I'm certainly not saying there's no white trash there (I'd never make that claim), but the popular image of the state is horribly distorted. Nitro is a small town in the suburbs of Charleston. A hundred thousand people live around there, including more than a few yuppies; it's far from being a remote area that can only be reached on foot. Sheesh.

— Sometimes I lie awake at night worrying that this website isn't nearly self-indulgent enough, so I'm going to purchase a digital camera this weekend. Now you'll be able to see what I'm having for dinner! Prepare yourselves for a new era, my friends.

— Speaking of dinner, we decided to have pizza last night, and I stopped to pick it up on my way home from work. I got there a little early, and they told me it would probably be another ten minutes before it was done. So, to kill time, I walked down the way to a little record store. I was perusing their fine selection of magazines, when I spotted a review of TheWVSR.com in an issue of Broken Pencil. Cool, I thought; I had no idea the review even existed. Yeah, they hated it. I'm apparently the web equivalent of Dude, Where's My Car? But damn, the pizza was good. That shit rocked.

August 27, 2001

Our trip to West Virginia went as smoothly as could be expected, even though we ran out of time and weren't able to see everyone we had wanted to see. I tend to make impossibly long lists (I'm an obsessive list-maker, which is a sure sign of mental illness) of things I want to do during trips, and almost always come away feeling mildly unfulfilled when we return home with a few of the items not crossed off. This trip was no different, even though it wasn't really my fault. All of our evenings were completely maxed-out with various family members stopping by to visit, and consequently we were unable to get together with my old partner in crime, Bill. I've known Bill since before elementary school, and we've got ourselves into enough trouble through the years to fill a dozen John Hughes movies, a couple episodes of Ripley's Believe It or Not, and several Bukowski novels. It doesn't feel natural to be in West Virginia and not see him, so that part sucked. But beyond that one major flaw, it wasn't a bad trip.

So, with no further delay, here's part one of A Few Things That Happened on Our Summer Vacation…

— We had intended to cook chicken on the grill the night before we left, so Toney had taken the meat out of the freezer early that morning to thaw. It was lying on the counter changing colors throughout the day, and putting out some kind of nasty liquid, so we decided we'd just order a pizza instead. But what to do with the chicken? We couldn't just leave it in the trash while we were gone; it would stink like an open grave, and probably trigger a vermin rave in our garage. We had to get it away from the house. So Toney tied it up in a plastic grocery bag, and we made plans to fling it into a dumpster on our way out of town. When we got up Sunday morning the bag was really "juicy" and was putting off a high funk. I didn't want that shit in our car, so I tied it to the driver's side window. And we drove through town with a rancid bag of chicken bouncing off our door, drizzling poison poultry juice across the landscape. A perfect start.

— We stopped for the first of our three visits to Cracker Barrel about an hour into the trip, and had my all-time favorite, the "Old-Timer's Breakfast." Here's a tip for ya: when ordering this meal, refer to it as the Alzheimer's breakfast. Waitresses seem to love this.

— Before leaving The Barrel, I found a bag of Jelly Bellies in the general store comprised of "rookie flavors." Supposedly it was all new flavors of jelly beans they were trying out, as sort of a test-market I suppose. They already make some freaky varieties of those things (like cantaloupe), so I couldn't imagine what was inside that bag. I had to have it. Toney was driving during this leg of the trip, and I sat in the passenger seat doling out bizarre jelly beans for comment and review. Some were so gross they literally made us gasp. At a gas station in Maryland, Toney bit into a white one and her face contorted before she almost instantly hocked the half-chewed glob onto the pavement an inch from my feet. You don't really see women spitting often enough these days. We foolishly tossed the little booklet that listed the flavors so we may be a little off on a few of these, but here's a partial list of what we think we were eating: sauerkraut, old vacuum cleaner bags, tin, blackened sea bass, table salt, scotch, bleu cheese, and kerosene.

— My parents' house is perfect. There's not a single blade of grass out of order, and not a speck of dust anywhere inside. It makes me feel like a slob. I bet they've never driven through town with a sack of chicken on their door. When I start wringing my hands about my feelings of inadequacy, Toney tried to reassure me that they're retired and have more time to work on such things. But it's always been this way, even when they were both working full-time and raising two lunatic kids. No, there's no getting around it, I'm a slob alright.

— As usual, there was a virtual buffet of excellent foods available 'round the clock while we were there. It's like being on a cruise ship passing through Appalachia, if you can imagine that. My mom always makes sure to cook up a giant pot of "half-runner" green beans when we visit, which are a WV delicacy that the Jelly Belly people really need to take a look at. I love half-runners, with onions and a little vinegar. Yum. I read somewhere that people have tried to raise them in California and other places and they won't grow, which is the way it's supposed to be. The rest of the country doesn't deserve half-runner beans. Also for lunch one day, for my benefit I'm sure, we had another local favorite: hot baloney! West Virginia round steak. It's thick sliced bologna, fried in barbecue sauce and eaten as a sandwich with lettuce, tomato, and onion. There's nothing better, I'm not joking.

— The clock in the bedroom we slept in sizzled. It sounded like bacon frying. I told my parents about it, but they said they couldn't hear anything. Hey, whatever. It sizzled. It's probably sizzling right now.

— My twentieth high school class reunion was going on the same weekend we arrived in town, but I didn't go. For some reason I had little interest in it. Bill went, and was reportedly the life of the party. Of course I would expect nothing less. After it was over I had a mild feeling of regret, especially after hearing about all the fun Bill had. Toney said something about a mid-life crisis, which didn't help anything. Not one little thing.

August 28, 2001

And now, part two of What We Did on Our Summer Vacation:

— Whenever we visit West Virginia various aunts, and a smattering of uncles, stop by to visit and ask how I like my job, and how we like Pennsylvania, and that sort of thing. It's a nice gesture that I wonder if I would put forth if the roles were reversed. I doubt if it would even occur to me, to tell the truth. Outside of a room where draft beer is available for purchase, I have few social skills. Anyway, Monday or Tuesday night while we were having dinner, one of my aunts suddenly had a pained look on her face, and stood up and excused herself. We continued to eat, and just as she left the room we heard, "Smack! ...Slap-Smack!!...Pop Pop...Slappety-Pop!" It was like the sound a roller coaster makes when it's coming back into the station. She had apparently left the dinner table to release a little urgent excess gas, and didn't quite make it to a secure location. Of course, everybody at the table just about choked on their food laughing, but trying to keep it quiet. By the time she returned, we had all summoned up enough inner strength to be wearing our game faces, and not a word was spoken about it. Until she went home.

— One afternoon my parents and Toney and I went to a place called Rock Lake. It used to be an incredibly cool swimming pool, surrounded by big rock cliffs and featuring trapezes and trampolines and shit — not to mention one of the longest slides I've ever seen. It's been around forever; my parents used to go there when they were kids. Not that this has anything to do with the story, but when I was young they wouldn't let black people swim there. The owners were adamant about it. When the government told them to change their policy, or face a forced shut-down, they closed the place! But I digress… The pool has been out of operation for a couple of decades now, and had fallen into disrepair. A few years ago somebody bought it, filled in the pool area and turned everything into one of those big entertainment complexes for kids: miniature golf, go-karts, arcade, noisy birthday parties, etc. etc. I had heard they did a good job with it, and had wanted to check it out. While we were there I asked Toney if she wanted to play laser tag. She looked at me like, "Are you out of your mind?" But after some coaxing, she finally agreed. My parents (and another aunt) just sat in the background laughing at us. But it was fun. I had to adjust the straps on my electronic vest to its fullest expansion to fit around my ample trunk, but after that it was smooth sailing. We kicked some eleven year old ass. Don't even think about messing with the laser masters, boys and girls! I'm almost sure I only thought that, and didn't scream it out loud.

— Another afternoon Toney and I went to lunch and a movie. We never go to movies unless we're on vacation. The last one we saw was Almost Famous, last October in Myrtle Beach. I had picked that one and Toney didn't like it much, so she insisted on picking this one. We saw Legally Blonde, and it was really funny. The next one we see probably hasn't been made or written yet, but I'm looking forward to it.

— I think it's just that time of year, but everywhere we went there were friggin' gnats and mosquitoes. If you stood in one place outside for any amount of time, you'd have tiny bugs crawling on your skin and making weird buzzing sounds in your ears. I was convinced they were laying eggs in my face, but I guess everything's OK. When I was a kid, they used to have trucks that drove up and down the streets cranking out huge billowing clouds of yellow poison to kill the bugs (we used to follow it on our bikes, riding inside the toxic cloud!), but I think the environmentalists put an end to that. Don Henley and his pals have made the world safe for pests and parasites, thank God.

— Wednesday afternoon Toney and I met my old friend Tim and his wife at Cracker Barrel. We talked about a million little things as our wives sat there looking mildly disgusted. It was a good time, but afterwards he insisted on picking up the check. I told him I didn't want somebody else paying for my dumplings, and he said, "I've been paying for your dumplings one way or the other all my life." I'm not sure what that means, but don't think it's a compliment.

— After I left Dunbar, I went to Nitro to check out the cloning clinic that's been in the news lately. It's in the old high school, which is now being used for many purposes. There's a daycare center, a church(?!), a few offices, and the Nitro police department, among other things. But all this stuff is on the first floor, and I was looking for Room 201 which I assumed was on the second floor. I walked confidently, like I did years ago in pursuit of those underage brewskis, and went up the steps. There was nobody around, and it was pretty damn spooky up there. Trespassing in long dimly-lit hallways with the knowledge of bizarre medical experiments taking place on the premises, adds up to a memorable experience. And it didn't help that I'm reading a Dean Koontz book. I half expected some horribly mutated man-beast to jump out and rip my spine out with its curved claws. But I soldiered on, and finally found Room 201. There was white paper over the little window in the door, and it was locked. I snapped a quick photo, then immediately heard footsteps. It sounded like somebody was coming up the steps! I got out of there. I'm glad none of my laser-tag victims were there to witness my pathetic display of cowardice. But, holy shit, my heart was pounding.

— The next morning we left, and drove forever back to the upper right-hand corner of Pennsylvania. It was a really good trip. One thing living in Scranton does, is make you see the good side of everywhere else. Charleston, WV is like friggin' Malibu compared to Scranton. But it's a cool place, even without the comparisons. When I left there ten or twelve years ago unemployment was really high, and the area was pretty depressed. But it's not like that anymore. It's thriving and bustling now. It's a comforting thing to see.

As we neared home, in need of a good ass-kneading, I started worrying that we'd find an empty lot with only a black smoldering square where our house used to be, and maybe a chimney standing by itself. I always think our house is going to burn down while we're away. Another sign of mental illness, I'm sure. But it was still standing, and the next day I ran over a big pile of dogshit with the lawnmower. For some reason it smelled like peanut butter. Odd.

Yes, the vacation was over.

August 31, 2001

— One of Toney's friends was born and raised in Charleston, SC, but she reportedly doesn't have even a trace of a Southern accent. Toney asked her about it a few days ago, and she said her father forbade his kids from adopting Southern speech patterns. She said he'd make them sit on the front porch and repeatedly say words correctly, if he ever heard them speak "Southern." His theory is that people instantly think you're stupid if they know you're from the South — and he's from South Carolina. Of course he's right, but I still don't like it.

— Have you ever seen a person drinking coffee at Taco Bell? Me either.

— Toney ripped out a page from a magazine she reads and left it by my computer for me to read. It's letters from readers telling about embarrassing moments, and here's the one she highlighted: *At my son's kindergarten orientation, the children and parents were sitting in a big circle in the gym. As an icebreaker, the principal asked the kids to say something about their parents. Some told what their parents did for a living, others told about parental or family hobbies, still others described their parents in general as "nice" or "fun." I was waiting for something along those lines. Instead, when it came around to us, my son said in a cheerful voice, "My daddy's a big fat man!"*

I have seen the future.

— There's nothing funny about this final piece, in fact it makes me want to cry. Through my vast network of spies and back-stabbers, I have obtained a copy of one of New York Mets catcher Mike Piazza's paychecks. Yes, he receives a paycheck every two weeks just like the rest of us — but the similarities end there. This is a West Virginia Surf Report world exclusive — it isn't stolen from another website. Don't even ask where I got it; we serious journalists will go to our graves protecting our sources.

Have a nice three-day weekend. See ya next week.

September 4, 2001

— Friday was completely insane. The Mike Piazza paycheck that I posted here was picked up and linked by a couple of high-traffic weblogs, and the resulting flood of visitors to my humble little village of filth was an exciting and scary thing to witness. As I clicked REFRESH on my stats page, and watched the numbers pile up faster than ass zits on a Dungeons and Dragons enthusiast I started getting nervous. Could I get in trouble for this shit? Would Piazza or the Mets unleash a team of ball-busting lawyers on my ass? Would my butthole become a tourist attraction behind prison walls? (It always comes down to that in the end…society's great deterrent.)

I fired off several emails to people I trust, asking for an opinion, and their feelings were almost unanimous: take it down! One friend works in a law office, and he asked an attorney about it. Take it down, was the word that came back. Another friend works in another law office in another state, and he did some research and felt I better take it down as well. A third said I was "playing around with some federal shit," and seemed disgusted that I was stupid enough to put it up in the first place. Holy shit, what had I done? The number of visitors just kept getting higher and higher and higher. I was sweating like a bull moose and was checking my email constantly, fully expecting someone from the Mets legal department to order me to cease and desist.

But nothing happened, at least not yet. In the heat of the moment I decided to pull the damn thing off the site, then almost immediately changed my mind. Everything incriminating is X'd out, after all, and anyone with a calculator could figure out how much Mike Piazza's two-week bring-home pay would be. His salary is public knowledge, right? I decided to take my chances, but continued to be nervous.

Friday night Toney and I were sitting on the couch watching TV when a car pulled into our driveway, with authority, and turned off its headlights. I started whimpering like a schoolgirl: "They're here! Sweet Jesus, they've come for me!!" I looked around for someplace to hide, but my wife abandoned me in my hour of need and I was left to deal with the Secret Service by myself. "Hi, I'm Andrew's Daddy!" the man said cheerfully as he made his way to our door. "Um, I think you have the wrong house," I mumbled, then collapsed in a chair. Holy hell.

The following day the number of visitors fell off dramatically, then even more dramatically on Sunday. By yesterday things were back to normal, and I'm not nearly as nervous anymore. I guess it could still happen, but I think the moment has passed. But check this out; here are the number of visitors TheWVSR.com received last week:

Monday 1312

Tuesday 1319

Wednesday 1046

Thursday 949

Friday 29,580

What a trip.

— As the number of visitors continues to level off after the madness of Friday it occurs to me that far more people would rather look at a professional baseball player's banking than read my observations and opinions. As it should be, I suppose.

— Yesterday Toney and I celebrated our eighth wedding anniversary, by not celebrating. I think eight is the no-acknowledgment-to-speak-of anniversary, and we're nothing if not traditionalists. We've been together for more than ten years now, and I feel in my bones that I'm with the right person. And that's a good feeling to have.

And that's all I have time for today, kiddies. Unless I'm arrested, I'll be back on Wednesday or Thursday. Have fun.

September 7, 2001

You can go ahead and start calling me a pussling now, 'cause I took the Piazza check down last night. When this thing started, and my friends voiced their disbelief in unison at my mammoth stupidity for posting it in the first place, I told myself I'd leave it up until someone asked me to take it down. And that has happened. A "friend" of Piazza's wrote and asked me semi-politely (with a distinct whiff of threat), to remove the check, citing privacy issues. After a few emails back and forth, I became reasonably convinced she was the genuine article, and not just Mark Maynard messing with me again. So I took it down. It was giving me an ulcer anyway. Too many people accessing the site through shady scrambling filters, and via unknown ISP's with grim and imposing names — and for all the wrong reasons. Oh, I'm obviously not above a cheap stunt here and there, but when the public speaks, and they say "we prefer looking at a baseball player's banking papers to your writing at a ratio of roughly 45,000 to 1," it can get you down if you're not careful. Plus it just made me nervous, and didn't serve any real purpose. This is supposed to be a humor site after all, not the poor man's Smoking Gun. So screw it. I took it down, and that's enough on that subject. Shit, I'm starting to feel like Lenny Bruce in those old grainy films they used to show on Night Flight, where he went on stage and just read transcripts from his court appearances. Completely batshit and obsessive. Screw it…I need to get back to my roots. I need to spend the weekend writing shit jokes. Lots of shit and dick jokes to get the taste back in my mouth.

September 9, 2001

— A lot has happened on the Piazza front during the last 36 hours. Some of it I'm not going to talk about right now, but let's just say I've had some very interesting conversations with people I never could've imagined I'd be talking to. This thing is becoming a mini-phenomenon. Morning DJs around the country are talking about it, and it's buzzing like a mofo around the Internet. There's a sizable discussion about it on the official Mets website, and I've heard rumors of a newspaper article in New Jersey (although I've been unable to confirm). The moment I took the check down, other (very) well-known sites started contacting me about possibly acquiring it. (Ha!) Obviously they want it for their own sites, which tells me they have no qualms, legally speaking, about putting it up. In addition, other sites have lifted it from me already, and are soaking up the extra traffic this stupid slip of paper continues to generate — beyond comprehension. This kind of thing doesn't happen too often, at least not to me. And that's why I decided to put the check back up. If I go to prison, I go to prison. ("What're you in for?" "Posting Mike Piazza's paycheck on the Internet." "Spread 'em, bitch.") I know I probably seem a little crazy right now, but I've never dealt with anything like this. It goes way beyond trying to decide on the four-roll pack of toilet paper, and the eight-roll, which is the normal caliber of decision I'm forced to make from day to day. Of course, at this point that wouldn't be difficult at all: the more the better is what I need. Sweet Maria!

— There's disturbing news today that Toney's mother may be coming for an extended visit in October/November. She's going to take a friggin' bus from Reno, because she's afraid to fly. I'd be more afraid of what might flop down beside me on one of those elongated trollies of despair, but that's just me. Anyway, she's planning on staying for about a month. Yes, a month. Thirty or so days of hearing her crackpot opinions on every subject, and interfering with our lives... Thirty or so days of moodiness and attitude... Thirty or so days of behind-my-back criticism to my wife... It's going to be grand.

— When we were in West Virginia a few weeks ago we went looking at tent trailers again, at a big-ass RV place near Huntington. Just for kicks we went into some of those giant tour-bus deals, and the kind of trailers you have to pull with a military vehicle or something along those lines. Absolutely amazing. One we saw costs $149,000! They're like rolling luxury apartments, I'm not kidding. Big-screen TVs, satellite dishes, recliners, upstairs bedrooms… Incredible. My Mom told me that some even have fireplaces. That blows my beleaguered mind. What was particularly cool (to me, anyway) was the seatbelts on the recliners and couches, and the little TV that shows the driver what's going on behind the trailer while on the road. That's my kind of roughing it, baby.

— Toney and I are considering buying a dog. We have one on-hold at the humane society right now, awaiting approval of our application(?!). It's a Jack Russell terrier/border collie combo package, and it's a three month old male — black and white. I have mixed feelings about all this, but it could be cool, I guess. I like dogs, I just don't like all the maintenance they require. We're still teetering back and forth, so there's a good chance we'll just say forget it. But we'll see. In the meantime, we went to PetSmart yesterday, and it was complete mayhem. Friggin' dogs were walking around that store, barking and spraying urine everywhere. One, the size of a full-grown deer, was wearing a sun-visor (I shit you not) and pulling his frightened-looking "master" around the joint. Birds were flying around. It was insane. And I couldn't believe my eyes when I saw a silly-ass contraption on the shelf that's supposed to serve as a doggie car seat. It was sorta like a child's car seat, modified, you know, for a dog. The picture on the front of a German Shepherd sitting up in one of those ridiculous things made me bust out laughing. I'm not sure I want to become indoctrinated into that particular culture. Ya know?

Stay tuned…

September 11, 2001

— Like most people, I'm pretty much desensitized to tragedy, and generally don't hesitate to make light of even the worst happenings. And I also have a deep dislike for the faux hyper-compassion of the Oprah Nation ("Won't somebody please think of the children?!"), but I feel sick to my stomach about what happened in New York and Washington today. A few things that have struck me, especially:

— Reports of helpless faces looking out windows of the World Trade Center, just seconds before the huge towers came down like curtains, presumably killing thousands. Absolutely horrifying.

— The fact that they have Bush in the air and in underground bunkers, which says that the President isn't safe on the soil of the United States. How is that even possible?

— I heard on the radio that a man was barricaded inside a bathroom of the airliner that crashed near Pittsburgh, on his cell phone reporting the hijacking when it went down. Can you even imagine being in that situation? The guy was probably on a business trip. He could've been looking at USA Today and sipping a cup of Starbucks just minutes before.

— Mayor Giuliani announcing at a press conference that kids are being kept at school, and will be sent to a centralized shelter if their parents don't show up at the end of the day. Gulp.

— Reports that the terrorists hijacked planes headed to California because they carried the most fuel, and would cause a more deadly explosion.

— The World Trade Center was there this morning, but now it's gone. It's gone!

— Footage of Palestinians celebrating in the streets because of the good news coming out of America today.

I've also heard people begin with the crackpot theories already, that the government was involved (to somehow stimulate the economy, if you can believe that load of utter bullshit), as well as the usual blame heaped on the President by people who oppose his politics. So tiresome.

I feel like a family member is gravely ill: really sad and also nervous in my gut about what's around the corner. For some reason you're now supposed to feel guilty about desiring revenge, but I hope they flatten whoever is responsible. Somebody has to pay, big time. And I don't feel guilty at all.

And now we're just watching the news networks report the same things over and over again, and we'll undoubtedly be here until bedtime. What else is there to do, really?

September 13, 2001

Here's part of an email I received from a friend who was in NYC the day of the attack:

Michele and I were in New York City this past weekend for a film festival promoting our documentary. We were scheduled to fly out of LaGuardia on Monday evening but due to an intensely active thunderstorm, our flight was canceled and a subsequent later flight was also canceled. We were forced to get a room at a hotel in Queens for the night. Bored, we went to a local bar where many who were also delayed had gathered. Most of the crowd was made up of flight attendants also waiting out the storm. We shared a beer with a talkative local who turned out to be a 20 year FDNY vet who had the night off. The next morning we got up at 5:00am to rush to the airport.

It was a beautiful cool morning as the storm the night before cleared out the hot and humid airmass we had been dealing with all weekend. Our flight took off at 6:55am and as we banked around lower Manhattan, I had an excellent view of the skyline and remarked to Michele what a nice, unexpected view it was as we usually get exit row seats over the wing and rarely get a clear view of the city (Michele, who gets nervous on take-offs, did not respond and kept her eyes tightly shut).

The rest of the flight was smooth and uneventful and we arrived at RDU early. My father picked us up at the airport at 8:45am. We traveled home with the radio off so we could talk about the trip. We arrived home with the phone ringing. My mother was frantically telling us to turn on the TV.

The rest everyone knows.

Three friends that I had traveled to New York with were not scheduled to leave until later that day. They are safe, but still in NYC. Jay and Gretchen (brother and sister) were enjoying their first-ever trip to NYC and staying in a friend's apartment in Greenwich Village, now part of the cordoned off area of the city below 14th street. The one thing they told me they wanted to do above anything else while they were in the city was to visit the World Trade Center observatory…they were either going to do it on Monday or Tuesday. They chose Monday pretty much at the last minute so it wouldn't interfere with their travel plans on Tuesday evening. They kept their ticket stubs.

The events of the past two days have been hard to comprehend, but as I am looking over this story it is the irony and close-calls of the days and hours leading up to this life-changing moment that strike me the most right now. It appears that the next weeks, months and years will be radically different than the ones that came before it.

September 17, 2001

— During times of trouble, when things are darkest, we naturally turn to the wisest among us for guidance and counsel. We seek their wisdom and support, to help make sense of the insanity around us, and to provide a clear-headed course for the future. Considering this, I can't tell you how glad I was to read the words below. It was as if the black clouds of despair instantly parted, and the sun was finally able to shine through…

New Yorker Whoopi Goldberg has called for restraint in the wake of the disaster until authorities are certain who is behind the attack. She says: "We have no choice but to wait and make sure because of the magnitude of the response. We're pretty much talking about taking out a country."

I think it's safe to say I haven't enjoyed this level of social clarity since before we lost Ted Knight.

— I spoke briefly with Toney's mother Sunday morning, and she said, "I keep expecting to see Chandra Levy's mother run out of the crowd, with that crying husband hanging off her shirt tail, waving a picture and screaming, "Don't forget about Chandra! Don't forget about Chandra!!" Wow. I was appalled. You know, after I stopped laughing.

— I read that it took America fifty-five days to respond to the attack on Pearl Harbor. Fifty-five days before that war mongering FDR launched his racist attacks on the misunderstood Japanese and Germans. And you can just imagine the disgusting level of patriotism, I mean nationalism, that must've been going on back then. How crass and insensitive we were to go out and win World War II! I'm so ashamed.

— A woman from the town where we now live was killed in Tuesday's attack in NYC, and one of her friends appeared on the local news proclaiming that she was always full of vim and vinegar. I'm not sure what her hygiene regimen has to do with anything, but whatever.

— The whole Piazza brouhaha seems pretty inconsequential right about now, huh? How was that ever important?

See ya in a day or two.

September 18, 2001

— I'm going to try to ease back on the terrorist bombing stuff from here on out. Everybody's talking about it, probably even dead people at seances and dogs at the park, so there's little need for my cockeyed analysis and opinions on the subject. I certainly won't be ignoring what's going on — I'm a news junkie — but I'd like this site to be fun, and a little different from what you find elsewhere. So I'll leave the political and sociological commentary to the experts, and get back to whining about my personal life. Like Carrot Top says, you've got to find the thing you're best at, and stick with it.

— An excerpt from an IM conversation I had with my brother a few days ago:

Him: Remember how you used to eat Funyuns, then blow your breath on me?

Me: No.

Him: It used to piss me off.

— We now have a puppy named Andy and, so far, the experiment is going well. He seems to be extraordinarily smart, and about three-fourths house-broken already. On the rare occasion that he has shit on the rug, he's been considerate enough to make it a collection of dry mini-logs for easy clean-up. It's like picking up stones. Now that's a good dog! He's three month old and hasn't chewed up a thing. We don't even have to lock him up at night; he sleeps on a blanket beside our bed. I was telling my dad about how well he's doing, and we started talking about a dog we had when I was a kid, named Scooby. "I believe that dog was retarded," he said. The dog couldn't be trusted to roam the house without supervision, so my parents would put him in the utility room while everyone slept. The next morning they'd open the door over a big pile, causing a large circular smear of terrier waste. Every day before school my mom or dad would be in there mumbling curses under their breath as they scrubbed a fresh shit-arc and sopped up various lakes of pee that eventually rusted out the bottom of our washing machine. He also had wicked gas that could cause varnish to abandon a door, and suffered from severe skin problems and epilepsy. But we loved him, and it was a sad day when he went to shit behind that big door in the sky. I still have his collar somewhere.

— When we were at the Humane Society picking up our new pup, I tried not to look at the blackened smokestack sticking out of the roof. Horrifying. I wonder if the people who live around there have to wipe dog ash off their cars?

And that's all for now. Until next time…

September 21, 2001

— Several days ago Toney told me she saw something "really gross" at Wal-Mart. I asked her if it was a customer or an employee, but it turned out she was talking about an item on their shelves… specifically, microwave pork rinds. "Can you think of anything more disgusting?" she asked. Well, sure I can: maggots, mayonnaise, wet briefs contests, Hillary Clinton, gumbo day at the hare-lip camp… But I got her point. Microwave pork rinds (or, as they call them down south, "cracklins"), hmm… that is pretty disgusting. A big bag of piping hot strips of rendered out pork fat packaged for convenience and speed?! Oh, I had to have some.

The next day I made a special trip to Wal-Mart, and purchased a three pack box. They were in the microwave popcorn section, and the packaging promised "a hot new snack that's convenient, crispy, and cracklin'." Yep, just what the doctor ordered. But they sat around unopened on our kitchen counter for a week or so as rescue workers in NYC pulled charred bodies out of a mountain of rubble, and my interest in a steaming bowl of crispy fat waned dramatically. Last night I took a deep breath though, and stepped up to the plate. The day of pork reckoning had arrived.

They come in a bag, like microwave popcorn, and the directions say to nuke them until the bag stops expanding. Right away my stomach started gurgling at the thought of the bag's contents expanding. Shit! And when I ripped the plastic off, I was smacked in the face by a wave of funk like evening feet and livestock semen. I tossed the bag inside the microwave, and hit the "popcorn" button. The bag leapt to life and immediately began jerking and puffing up. There was a pronounced sizzling sound coming from inside, and the stink grew progressively worse as the sizzling got louder. At this point Toney was yelling because of the horrible smell, and waving her hands at the air and distorting her face. It was like a crematorium in there.

When I opened the microwave I very nearly vomited, and I'm not just being dramatic. I've never smelled anything quite like what rushed out from behind that door, and my gag reflex kicked in. I stepped back to regain my composure, and to let things settle down a bit — the greasy pork pouch was smoking and sizzling like a bitch. What the hell was I doing, anyway?! Toney had fled the scene by this time, and I was all alone with my foul-smelling sack of cracklins. After a while I transferred them to a bowl, and went downstairs to try to summon up enough courage to eat one of the scary-ass things.

They were popping and whistling and carrying on in the bowl, and I was afraid to look directly at them for fear I might be blinded by splattering fat. The whistling concerned me too. Eventually I picked one up, eyed it, and bit off a corner. Surprisingly, it wasn't too bad. Sort of a bacon/Rice Krispies deal, pleasantly salty. Interesting, I thought. I ended up eating five or six, and tossed the rest in the trash. They taste a lot better than they smell, but afterwards it felt like the inside of my mouth was treated with an underbody rust inhibitor; there's a hell of a lot of grease. I won't be buying the horrifying things again, but truthfully they weren't as bad as I'd expected — once you get past the smells of the Nazi death camps. Plus, you just know they're made from skin and snouts and scrotums and buttholes, and various other slaughter house scraps. Call me common if you'd like, but I think I'll just stick with potato chips.

— A couple of recent events have nudged me ever closer to my coming mid-life crisis.

A few days ago I was bitching about a poorly-designed spreadsheet at work, and blurted, "Goddamn, you've got to be Mannix to figure this thing out!" When I looked up everyone was staring at me like I'd just lapsed into the language of the silver-tipped barn owl. "Who or what is a Mannix?," they were thinking. I was sickened to realize I was the oldest person in the room, and making obscure old-fart references that have no meaning to anyone born after the Johnson administration. I may as well put on a raccoon coat, honk a big brass horn, and shout, "23-Skidoo!"

When I was picking up a pizza earlier in the week, there was a group of teenagers taking up three or four booths just inside the door of the restaurant. They were being pretty loud, like you'd expect, and most of the guys were wearing giant pants that wouldn't even be tight on me, with about a yard of underwear sticking out of the top. There was a lot of earrings and dyed hair and attitude: all very typical and familiar. On my way out, I accidentally bumped the foot of one of the big-pants enthusiasts with my free 2-liter bottle of root beer. I thought, oh shit, here comes trouble. But there was no trouble. He looked at me with a nervous expression and said, "Excuse me, sir." And I was horrified as they all regarded me with respect, like I was their freakin' principal or something. Sir. Ha!

I'm leaning more towards a Camaro, instead of a Corvette. I've always felt that Camaros have more balls. And I'm seriously considering taking up the guitar; chicks dig the guitar. Hell, yeah. I'm not done living yet, baby! It's gonna be the cat's meow.

Have a great weekend! Keep saving your bacon grease, and don't forget to buy war bonds to help out our men and women in uniform. See ya on Monday.

September 24, 2001

— I mentioned a while back that when I step up on the bathroom scales you can see sparks inside the little window, as the wheel is forced into a violent spin and is ultimately wrenched off it axis by the sheer power of the centrifugal pull. It whirs and whirs and whirs, and always comes to a stop at 230 pounds. 230! When I worked at Peaches in Greensboro years ago, I briefly ballooned to 200 (I remember, because I was horrified), and the store director said, "Damn Jeff, you're getting a fat ass; you look like a woman from behind." Yes, the love I felt in those days was immense, but I often wonder what he'd say today, about the state of my fat ass, after the equivalent of an extra two or three newborn babies have been added to the mix? Most of the time I don't really care one way or the other, but every once in a while a little self-respect bubbles to the surface and makes me want to try and reduce the payload a little. Three weeks or so ago I decided to make another conscious effort to watch what I eat, and only drink beer on weekends, and walk a couple of miles around the track after dinner. I did pretty well at sticking to all the rules, and felt good about my progress. My pants felt looser, and I was energized. I was drinking water instead of soda, eating skimpy little turkey sandwiches instead of big ol' greasy burgers, and consuming pussified quantities of Yuengling. Before dark every evening I'd walk over to the school by our house, and hoof it around the track for forty-five minutes with all the other neighborhood fatties. And now the results are in! 230.

— Last week a friend forwarded me one of those gag emails about all the different types of shits people take at work. You know, like the Stealth Shit, and the Hit and Run, and the Bombadier — I'm sure you're familiar with the concept. It was mildly amusing, but the conversation we had afterwards was the best part. I casually mentioned that I've never taken a crap at work. Not once. To my surprise, this seemed to shock him. He was absolutely incredulous. Am I the freak here? I can't even imagine taking a dump amongst other members of the human race, especially co-workers. I see those guys who proudly tuck a newspaper under their arm, and march into the bathroom as if their off to defend our freedoms, and I think they're the freaks. I go into the men's room to wash my hands, and there's sounds coming out of the corner stall like somebody's practicing the clarinet, and I just shake my head. Like George Costanza, I require an adequate buffer zone, and I guess I've trained my system not to even put in that particular request between the hours of nine and six. It never occurred to me that I may be in the minority here. My friend thinks I must be some kind of otherworld cyborg, or something. "How do you hold it!?" he screamed across long-distance phone lines, "Not once?! I'm in the hundreds here!!"

— Saturday afternoon I decided to walk over to the now-open State Street Bar and Grill, which rose from the ashes of the late, great John K's Pub —

which was shut down a few months back by those pussies down at the Department of Public Health. It's been open now for a few weeks but I haven't really had a burning desire to go in, judging from all the renovations and upgrades they've done to the outside. Most of the squalor that was the essence of John K's has been replaced by nice landscaping and outdoor seating and blonde wood and tasteful light fixtures. It's a sad thing to behold. Where the overflowing dumpster once sat is now a flower garden. It's not a corner bar anymore, it's a hangout for the young and upwardly mobile. But I attempted to set aside my deep-seated prejudices, and check things out with an open mind.

When I went in I was floored by all the changes. Where there was once filthy, rancid carpeting was now beautiful hardwood floors. The old bar was gone, and in its place was a giant, curved thing with fancy inlays and designs on its surface. There was track lighting, and framed black & white photographs that were more matte than photos. There were plants sitting around. Plants! And the clientele was well-dressed — most of the men in ties, and the women in dresses. I felt a little shabby in my shorts and tennis shoes, which would've been unthinkable in the old days. You could've gone in there wearing a turban of your own solid waste, and nobody would've blinked an eye. I was horrified. The place was crawling with goddamn yuppies. Packed with yuppies. I took a seat at the bar, the only one that was vacant, and ordered a pint of Yuengling. The bartender was friendly, and stood there and shot the shit for a few seconds, then left me alone with my beverage. I watched all the activity with amazement. Well-scrubbed cute-girls scurried about delivering plates of complex entrees to tables, and delivered orders to the bartenders for martinis and shit. What had happened here? Where were the hotdogs and pitchers of beer? I sat and drank another lager, then another, and started to soften a little. It wasn't that bad, in fact it was pretty nice. Everyone seemed friendly, which is something to make note of in northeastern Pennsylvania. And they still serve Yuengling in the same sized glasses, in the same building as before.

Why be such a snob? Then I offered to settle my tab, and found out the beers were only a buck seventy-five each! Hell, they were two twenty-five under the old regime. Screw John K's, a new era is upon us!

— Yesterday Toney and I went to a couple of open houses in our town, to see how the rich folks live. One of the places we went into had a shitload of taxidermy in it, including a big-ass moose head that practically filled a bedroom. It was frozen in time, forever looking to its right — undoubtedly at the hunter (the owner of the house?) who would end his life in the next couple of seconds. It gave me the creeps. I mean, what the hell? Why would anyone want a collection of traumatized animal heads in their house?

We also checked out a really nice place that had an awesome home-office in a loft overlooking the family room. It was cool as hell, but the place was listed at about a hundred grand more than what we paid for our house. And the depressing thing: the owners were younger than us. Bastards. Mr. and Mrs. Fancy-Pants probably stayed in college and took their careers seriously. Assholes.

Then we went to Target and heard a page over the loud speaker for "Edna Frogbutter" to please report to the dressing rooms. I swear to god. And I heard a woman come out of the bathrooms and tell her friend, "Damn, it sounded like a fountain in there." We checked out the Spongebob section, but it was just stuff for kids, which is blatant ageism in my opinion. They had a cool t-shirt that showed Spongebob "taking it around the town" which I would've gladly bought if they'd offered it in a husky-long. Their loss, I say. Afterwards we went to the grocery store, and I did my old trick of putting about twenty-seven eggplants in our cart while Toney wasn't looking. Some things are funny year after year after year.

And now it's time to go back to work… Why can't I just do this for a living?

September 26, 2001

— On a related note, I've received some interesting email about my recent admission that I've never, not even once, taken a crap at work. Yes, friends, that means the '70s, the 80s, the 90s, and the new millennium. I could bend a spoon with the power I have over my own colon ...or something. Anyway, here's the best of the lot, by far:

To describe my feelings (read "envy") of your ability to schedule crapping as desired, you might want to watch the movie "Unbreakable". Its about a guy (played by Samuel L. Jackson) who has been sickly and fragile his whole life. His only desire is to be super human. He knew that somewhere in the world there had to be a man that was an exact opposite of him, who never got sick, who never got hurt (Bruce Willis).

You are my Bruce Willis. My passion for avoiding work-place craps is just as powerful and just as passionate as yours. Yet, I cannot avoid it. My entire life I knew there had to be someone who was just the opposite, who could pencil in crap times on a calendar weeks ahead of time, and never suffer the humiliation of the work-place crap. You are that man Jeff Kay, and I am torn between envy and hatred (sort of like my feelings for John Holmes).

What makes it even more frustrating is you probably take this ability for granted, feeling no sense of appreciation for this power for which you have been blessed. Walk a mile in my wingtips bucko, and you would never look at colon control the same again.

We have a dinner table game we play every night at my house (this is no joke) called "Guess How Many Craps Daddy Had At Work Today". My only consolation is knowing you don't get to experience moments like this with your family.

In my eyes, you are the combination of Bruce Willis and John Holmes....I hate you....yet I cannot look away.

Thanks, Tim. Very nice, indeed.

October 5, 2001

— As of this writing I've lived in West Virginia, North Carolina, Georgia, California, and Pennsylvania, but as far as my co-workers are concerned, I'm a California Guy. Never mind that I only lived there for four of my thirty-eight years, it's the most exciting place on the list so that's where I'm from. Case closed. I'm not making fun of them (much), but I'd guess that seventy percent of the people in my office have never been west of the Mississippi, and a good number have never even been on an airplane. So that means the only California they know is the romanticized version from TV, the movies, and radio. And it also means I've got to be a major disappointment to them, since Brian Wilson didn't write too many songs about forty year old fat men who sit around eating peanuts in the shell and scouring the internet for pictures of people with their asses glued to toilet seats. There might be one or two from late in his career, but definitely no hit singles. Regardless, the fact that I moved here from the land of swimming pools and movie stars is never far from their minds. Most are either curious ("Do all the women out there really have big, fake tits?"), or defensive ("I'm sure the Snickers bars in the vending machines out in California are better than the ones we have here..."), but it's always simmering right under the surface. Earlier this week I came hobbling into work, because I'm a broken down old man on the cusp of a mid-life crisis, and a group of mustachioed loud-mouths asked what I'd done to myself. I told them my back was hurting again, and one replied, "Must be all that wild California-style sex!" And that instantly touched off an avalanche of roaring laughter that went on far longer than the quality of the joke warranted. California-style sex... yes, we'll probably never get the avocado stains out of the mattress... I just kept on hobbling, and didn't say anything else. We California Guys are cool like that.

— If you're in the market for fucked-upness (and who isn't?), check out your local Party City store. I went into one a few days ago, and the stuff on their shelves is downright bizarre. They're getting cranked up for

Halloween, and they've got items that I've never seen before, and could never imagine even if I quit my job and sat around trying. I saw a wall of masks that looked like heads of people who've been ripped apart by wild dingoes. And I checked out a wide array of strange makeup kits that help you create the illusion of a nest of spiders busting through your cheek…or a ballpoint pen plunged into your cranium… or a baseball driven deep into your former eye socket. They also have chest wigs (!?), plumber costumes, big ten-pound rubber rats, longshoreman hooks dripping in blood, and ten thousand other freaky items. Like Disneyland, it might require more than a single day to experience it all, but I highly recommend a visit or two.

— Speaking of Halloween, I want to dress up like a skeleton this year, but not a human skeleton. I want to be a donkey or horse skeleton. Do they make such a costume? Please let me know if you see one.

— Sometimes when it's slow at work I search around the internet for talk radio stations in foreign countries. I get tired of listening to domestic bitching all the time, so I seek out bitching from overseas. Right after the World Trade Center attacks I stumbled across a show from the UK hosted by a guy named Clive Bull, and now I'm completely addicted to it. It's a late night program out of London, that starts at four in the afternoon Scranton time. I'd never heard of Clive Bull (the station's website describes him as a "legend"), but he doesn't put up with much crap. He forces people to stay on topic, and won't let them get away with fuzzy logic or ideological spin. It's a really good show, and I've tuned in almost daily for three weeks or so. I'm to the point where I recognize some of the frequent callers, and know the London weather forecasts far better than the local ones. I'm up to speed on the internal debate over national ID cards and whether Britain should join the Euro, and have heard many Londoners' views on the U.S. War on Terrorism. It's enjoyable and addictive but… I think I'm picking up an accent. I've noticed myself adopting a new cadence to my speech, and it concerns me. Obviously it's OK for British people to talk British, but it's incredibly geeky for an American to do so. I may as well put on the Dungeons and Dragons robes, if I allow this to happen. If, in a couple of months, I start writing here that it's quite blowy out, and I had to wear a mac and rubbers to work, I beg of you to perform an intervention. Your help is needed, and appreciated.

— When we moved into our house a year and a half ago we bought a bunch of "five-year" light bulbs, and now they're all burning out. Bastards. I not only want my money back, but I also want some additional dollars, because my sense of trust has been destroyed forever. And I'm not sure I can continue to work, because of the severe mental anguish I've suffered. So they may have to pay my salary for the next thirty years too. This is bad, really bad. I'm on the verge of a complete breakdown.

— The results of our latest Surf Report mini-poll are in, and it appears that I am the freak here. People who've never shit at work make up only ten percent of the people who responded, while there was a tie for the top response: thirty percent said "Once in a while, I don't know what the big deal is," and "Only when there's no alternative." Hey, whatever. You people keep on crapping on stage like GG Allin, and I'll continue to do it in the comfort of my home, behind closed doors, and with towels stuffed under the door.

I'm mildly shocked at the results of the poll, but I have to admit that my way has its limitations. Years ago, when dinosaurs roamed the earth, I went to Charleston, SC with my girlfriend and her family for a long weekend. We stayed with a friend of their family, in a really nice house on an island off the South Carolina coast. I remember that the place was immaculate, and had wall-to-wall snow-white carpeting. I was terrified that I would flip a meatball off my plate onto the virgin rug, or track in railroad grease or something. I've been known to do that sort of thing. But I'm getting off track here....

When we got to the house I was distressed to see that the only bathroom was right off the kitchen(?!), which is where everyone hung out and drank cocktails. There was no other option than to try to "hold it" until we got back. Four days would be pushing things a bit, but I thought I could pull it off.

The first couple of days were a breeze, but then I started feeling sluggish. Eventually I became puffed up like the Michelin man, and was in a continuous state of distress. I kept looking at that bathroom (which was mocking me), and weighing my options. But I couldn't do it, not with four people standing just ten feet away. I'd simply have to tap into some unknown inner strength and see it though to the end.

One night, probably night three, my girlfriend and I went out and had a few drinks. And while we were driving around afterwards, we parked and one thing started leading to another. It was dark and we were in a secluded area, so we decided to climb into the backseat to continue the festivities. And that's when disaster struck. As I was trying to get over the seat, a loud sustained booming noise erupted from my body. It sounded like the Queen Mary had pulled into Charleston Bay. Or like somebody was practicing the bassoon nearby. A flock of sea birds took to the air out of fear for their safety. It caught me by complete surprise, and for a split second I was confused by the intrusive noise. But then I realized what had happened, and I wanted to crawl inside the glove compartment and pull up the door. Talk about a showstopper! If my girlfriend hadn't been such a good sport about it, I would've had myself a good cry right there on the spot.

The next day I discovered a second toilet in the corner of the garage, slipped away and took care of business in a tiny plywood room that was roughly the temperature of a jet engine inside. Afterwards I went back into the house, covered in sweat but walking on air. I felt like Fred Astaire, and I think I may have even twirled and kissed a few hands in an accelerated fit of enthusiasm.

So, you see, even the Colon Master has his limits.

— Jeff and Toney's Bed and Breakfast Inn and Old Country Tavern opens its doors for the season today. My parents will be here this weekend, followed by Toney's crazy mother (for a month!), and who knows after that? One thing's for sure, we're going to have a busy fourth quarter here at the Inn. Better get your reservations in now.

Have a great weekend!

October 11, 2001

— Suddenly it's fall. Just a couple of weeks ago neighbors were outside making lots of noise, wearing shorts and riding bikes, having barbecues and washing their cars. But just like that there's orange, red, and brown leaves all over our lawn, we've had to burrow deep into our hall closet to find jackets, and the smell of burning wood dominates the outside when the sun goes down. And all is quiet.

I love fall, it's my favorite time of year. Most people seem to prefer spring, but give me autumn any day. It's invigorating, and puts me in a good mood. I swear I could live in Portland or Seattle, someplace where's it's gloomy and rainy a lot of the time, with little problem. Well, all the Communists might be a problem, but you know what I mean. Even when I was a kid I remember loving cold overcast days; my parents made jokes about me being a lost member of the Addam's Family. It's been that way forever. Please feel free to psychoanalyze if you'd like.

— Since the leaves are changing and the temperatures are falling, I made the ceremonial first trip to the liquor store over the weekend for the traditional big ol' jug of fall whiskey. Forget about that stupid groundhog, the day Jeff Kay purchases bourbon is the true indicator that summer is officially over. I hardly ever drink liquor, but there's something about a good belt of booze when the leaves are falling. It tastes like the season, or the season tastes like the whiskey…or something like that. Or perhaps I'm just a drunk, making a pathetic stab at romanticizing my addiction? That's a possibility as well…

— My parents were here this past weekend, and it was a difficult adjustment to have visitors and not feel the urge to choke someone into a state of unconsciousness. Comparatively, at least, they're easy to get along with. (We'll get to experience the flipside in a few weeks when Toney's mother bursts through the door and starts spreading around her own unique brand of joy, but I'd rather not think about that right now...) They somehow know to stay out of your way when you need them to stay out of your way, and to help out when you'd like them to help out. I guess you could say they have common sense, and consideration for others. Yes, it was a jarringly foreign experience; we're just not used to that sort of thing around here.

On Sunday we went to a big pumpkin patch/Christmas tree farm close to our house, and took a hayride and drank apple cider and had some good clean country fun. The highlight was the corn maze, a big cornfield with trails carved into it. We went in, thinking it would be little more than a pleasant walk in the cool air, but then we couldn't find our way out. Man, oh man, somebody put some serious time into designing that thing; it seemed like there were a thousand overlapping paths, most leading to nowhere. We walked and walked, and passed the same things over and over again. It was like a Scooby Doo cartoon. We kept seeing the same people, and I thought I could detect expressions of escalating concern on their faces. Or maybe it was just me that was getting scared. I started wondering if anyone had a cell phone, in case we were still milling around in that bitch when the sun went down.

And then it started snowing. Yes, snowing. The skies grew dark, and big snowflakes began to fall. Toney said something about the Donner Party, which I tried to ignore, and my dad said the flakes were going down the back of his shirt collar, and making their way all the way to his belt. The wind started whipping up, it was incredibly cold, and we were lost in a giant cornfield with oblivious apple-eaters, the morbidly obese children of the corn. And I had to urinate like the proverbial racehorse.

Round and round we went, through the ten-foot tall cornstalks, the novelty long since worn off, until we finally found… the entrance. After an hour we were back to where we started! I asked the guy if there really was an exit, and he laughed and assured me there was. But we were in no mood to keep looking and went Out through the In door. Shit. A few more minutes and I probably would've freaked, and started thrashing my way through the walls. When it comes to building a corn maze, those people ain't half-steppin'.

— After our narrow escape I made a beeline to a row of small huts situated over a foamy pool of human waste. I opted to use the plastic urinal attached to the wall, so that I didn't have to stare down into the abyss, at the great wads of fudge-striped toilet paper bobbing around in the cess below. As I found sweet relief I was alarmed to hear a pronounced rush of liquid through a large pipe over my head, and on to places unknown. I was sure that everyone within twenty-five yards could hear the melody of my bodily fluids being whisked away by some insidious gravity-defying piss pump. When was this invented? My instincts told me to pinch it off and stop the roar immediately, but I quickly came to my senses. When I stepped out I must've had a look of disgust on my face because my dad said, "If you think those are bad, you should've seen the ones at the Putnam County Fair. They hadn't been sucked out in about a week, and were piled up almost to the seat. It was enough to gag a maggot." I guess he didn't hear.

— Sunday morning a couple of Mormons came to our door and I went into immediate defense mode. "We're getting ready to go out…to church, actually…we're devout Catholics…and we need to get ready for church…we're late for mass, or whatever…thanks for stopping by though…" Slam. My mom said, "Jeff, how many lies did you tell those men? They were religious."

— I've been reduced to "watching" the Braves - Astros playoff games on the internet at work, using the pitch by pitch feature on espn.com and cnnsi.com. It's a far from satisfying way of following a baseball game, repeatedly hitting REFRESH and reading that B.J. Surhoff was hit by a pitch. But I'll be damned if I'm going to pay the $9.95 Major League Baseball is charging for access to radio broadcasts via the internet, of the playoffs and World Series games. Wotta ripoff. They're on TV and radio for free, but you've gotta open up your wallet to listen through your computer? Where's the rationale? They run ads on the internet, Lord knows. I'd be interested in meeting someone who actually paid this fee. I'd like to interview them for the site.

Sorry it was so long between updates. Visitors always throw off the rhythm of my world, and I've been getting by on about four or five hours of sleep lately. Yesterday when I sat down to write this crap, it was like trying to squeeze out a little more toothpaste from a depleted tube. But I got a whopping six hours last night, so I'm rested and things are back to normal.

See ya on Monday.

October 15, 2001

— I had to spend twenty bucks on a new computer mouse yesterday. My old one developed a ball disorder, so I had to put it out to pasture. The same thing will probably happen to me someday, but I'll cross that bridge when I get to it. Anyway, I don't have a problem spending money on something that improves my world, like a new CD or something, but it pisses me off to have to spend money in order to bring things back to where they were yesterday. Ya know?

— I saw an ad in the paper saying they're gonna let people go through the frightening corn maze I mentioned here last time, after dark, with flashlights. I was fearing for my life in broad daylight, I'll be damned if I'm walking into that quagmire of fresh produce after the sun goes down. Who thought up this idea? Why the need to ratchet up the danger? It's as bad as backwards roller coasters…some things just shouldn't be messed with. My prediction is they'll find skeletons clutching flashlights next spring. I hope I'm wrong.

— As good as anything Christopher Guest and Eugene Levy could ever come up with is a local show, on Public Television up here, called Pennsylvania Polka. God, it's a riot. It's sorta like a geriatric version of American Bandstand, with loud wheezing accordions. When we first saw it we assumed it was old re-runs from the late '70s, based on the clothes the people were wearing. But the copyright date at the end told us we were wrong. Copyright 2000?! No friggin' way!

We've probably watched twenty episodes since we've been here, and the show is always worth a couple dozen belly laughs per week. It's fun to watch while having a few adult beverages, if you know what I mean. The host wears a toupee that is simply mind-boggling in its badness, and the band members look like they drive forklifts by day, and rock the polka circuit by night. Some of the "dancers" appear as if they've already died, but their partners just couldn't resist one last night on the town. Some have given up all pretense of dancing, and simply walk around. One old guy sashays about the dance floor with, I shit you not, a canister of oxygen strapped to his side. Old women are regularly seen dancing together, and they occasionally roll out a gentleman in a wheelchair, with hands curled up like a dinosaur and his head permanently cocked to the right. One week somebody had placed a sombrero on his head that was roughly four feet across.

I didn't think it was possible, but this past Saturday night's show actually surpassed any we'd seen before. I nearly shit myself laughing. They were doing some kind of craziness called a "broom dance," where a kitchen broom was supposed to be passed from person to person, for God knows what reason. But things went awry when a strange little woman got hold of the broom and refused to let go. People would be-bop over and attempt to take it from her, but she'd snatch it away and continue on with her spastic dance of dementia, a crazed smile plastered on her face. At one point a virtual tug-of-war broke out on the dance floor as somebody finally decided enough was enough, possibly the show's producers. I couldn't believe my eyes. She was howling like a wild animal. When they finally wrested the sacred item from her clutches, the toupee man rushed in and began dancing with her in a series of accelerated spins, probably to avoid violence. Several minutes later the couple danced past the camera, and she had that same wild expression frozen on her face, and the crazy smile. I couldn't catch my breath for a full minute after that.

Holy shit, I wish I had it on tape. I've seen a lot, but nothing quite like that.

October 17, 2001

— On August 1 Toney called me at work and asked me to stop on my way home and buy salt. Salt. Nobody runs out of salt. You buy one of those round, blue containers with the umbrella chick on it once, and use it for the rest of your life. I've never known anyone to actually deplete a box of salt. I'm pretty sure that in some families they're passed on from generation to generation, along with that little cup of toothpicks in the cabinet above the stove. But whatever...I do as I'm told. I'm nothing if not dutiful. But I'll be giving you occasional updates on how our renewed salt supply is holding out, and how many days have passed since we last purchased it. This is the kind of thing you can expect in the second year of TheWVSR.com. I'm toying with the idea of making this a pay site, by the way.

— I mentioned a few days ago that I've been listening to a British radio show every day, through my computer at work. The host is a guy (I'm sorry, a bloke) named Clive Bull, and he's really good. Plus, I'm just intrigued by the normal day to day lives of people in England. I've always had a fondness for England, for some reason, and you can't really get a sense of how things are in a place simply by staying in a hotel there for week. I like to listen to real people bitching about their doctors and discussing the London mayoral race, and to hear their views on the "war." I get off on the commercials as well. And I may be a pathetic sap, but I still think it's cool as hell to be able to sit in my office in Nowhere, USA, and listen to a radio show being broadcast on the other side of the world. Anyway, on Monday somebody sent Clive an email asking for his opinion on the Wonderbum, a newly invented undergarment for women that lifts and separates the butt cheeks. It's sorta like a Wonderbra for the ass. He laughed it off as a joke, and quickly dismissed it. He thought someone was pulling his leg. But it was real, I'd read an article about it earlier in the day. So…I found the piece and sent it to him by email, along with a short note. And, roughly five minutes after I hit SEND, he read it on the air! Made my day. People driving in their cars in London were hearing Clive Bull read a note that I'd typed in Scranton five minutes before. How cool is that?

— It's been 77 days since we last purchased salt.

— A friend and I were exchanging emails back and forth yesterday, talking about various subjects, and this was his final message in the series:

Well, let me see. In the last 4 minutes you've managed to trivialize a terrorist attack and ridicule a deaf man. You, sir, are in peak form, the likes of which haven't been seen since '79.

October 20, 2001

A few more things:

— When my parents visited a couple of weeks ago they brought us a trunk load of Cheerwine. In case you're unfamiliar with this regional favorite, it's an odd-tasting cherry-cola concoction that's popular (and produced) in North Carolina. Even though "wine" is in the name it's non-alcoholic; it's a mildly bizarre soft drink that you can purchase only in a tiny pocket of the South. It tastes a little like Dr. Pepper, but not really. It's more like Dr. Pepper after you've gargled with Plax. When I lived there I developed a fondness for the stuff, for whatever reason, and good ol' Mom and Dad remembered and picked me up a case on one of their many treks to Myrtle Beach. Man, I'd forgotten how sweet it is. I defy you to drink more than one can per day without spiraling into a diabetic coma. I'm not kidding, I may have to go shopping for an insulin pump by the time I make it through the twenty-four cans. Yeah, it's sweet, but it's good. Damn good. At least I think it is. Something way in the back of my mind is telling me it's really just shitty swill, and I'm romanticizing it because it's regional and hard to get. But I'm trying to suppress those thoughts, and just enjoy my case of soda. God, sometime I think I should just check myself into a hospital for a "rest"…

— I set our alarm for 6 AM today and it went off at 5:36. What would cause something like that to happen? Should I worry about it starting a fire?

— And finally, Rocky in the Insane Asylum has forwarded his review of the package of microwaveable pork rinds I sent him. He cooked them up at work, and spread around the pork goodness to his co-workers. Here ya go:

I knew, in the back of my mind, that these Microwave Pork Rinds would go over well where I work. Please keep in mind that I work at a state mental hospital in the middle of West Virginia where there is a fine line between employees and patients. (the employees wear badges and work less)

I was concerned about the warnings posted on the back of the bag, but figured what the hell. In the event of a tragedy, I could always blame a patient. I was quite aroused that it took only 60 seconds for the rinds to cook. The smell was no worse than the usual odors wafting from the cafeteria. I proceeded to take the bag-o-rinds around the hospital to see what the staff would think.

Jani, a switchboard operator, wouldn't try them. Slut. She asked what I was carrying around. "A digital camera," I replied. "Don't take my picture!" she said. "Don't worry, there's no film in the camera." Dumb slut.

Next I mosied toward the Security Office, Larry the Guard wouldn't try them at first, but John the Guard dove right in. Once Larry determined that I hadn't laced them with anything that would make his bowels instantly let loose, he tried them. They both loved them!!! They demanded to know where they could get some. I was lucky to leave the office with my bag intact.

I then ventured to the Training Department, where Melissa tried and liked the rinds. I'd do her. Queer boy Jerry the Trainer wouldn't try them. I wouldn't do him.

By this time the rinds were about spent. I decided that I needed to try one, and I did. While I'm not a big pork rind fan, these really weren't bad..

Thanks Jeff.

No, thank you, Rocky. I'm not ashamed to admit I wiped away a tiny tear while reading your report. The tenderness of the piece touched something deep inside my soul.

And that'll do it for me. I took a vacation day from work yesterday, and stayed away from the computer as much as possible. I needed to get my riffled ass out of the house for a change. I'm becoming a shut-in. A Cheerwine-swilling, rack-thinking shut-in. I needed to get out amongst some living, breathing people, and I'm going to try to do some more of that today. If I'm not careful, I'll end up reading science fiction novels, and quoting Monty Python in a British accent. And that's something I simply can't allow to happen.

See ya on Monday…or Tuesday.

October 23, 2001

— I made a conscious effort to live like a normal human being over the weekend, and stay away from this trance-inducing computer screen, and the 24/7 "war" coverage and all that entails. For whatever reason, I was feeling the need to interact with other human beings for a change, and go wading into the muddy waters of the community. Yes, it was an interesting experiment, but pretty much doomed to failure from the start. Who could've predicted that?

I took Friday off from work, because I damn well felt like it, and Toney and I went to lunch and browsed around a few stores. It sounded like a good idea in the abstract when we were planning it the night before, but when the reality of it hit, my heart just wasn't in it. I sleep like five hours a night anymore, because of my various mental illnesses (I look like Frank Torre now; the bags under my eyes could hold a head of cabbage each), and I'm generally exhausted and bitchy all the time. I was bitching up a storm Friday.

We went to Friendly's for lunch, and I stupidly ordered chicken quesadillas. Who orders Mexican food at a sandwich shop? Only your dumbass correspondent, that's who…and for good reason. As my reward for being such a fool, the waitress brought me a steaming platter of shit to eat. I think that's actually what she said: "OK ma'am, you ordered the Swiss mushroom burger and fries, and for you sir…a big steaming plate of shit to eat. Could I get you folks some mustard or anything?" The so-called chicken that was insinuated into the stinking mess she placed in front of me was the color of nickels, and as stringy as cat food. I hesitantly broke the seal on the pool of congealed grease, freed a wedge of dripping gloop, closed my eyes, and choked it down. It was as bad as it looked. It tasted like a dirty oven.

After a couple more death wedges I pushed the plate away and ordered a hot fudge sundae. I needed to get the taste out of my mouth, and quick. But the ice cream wasn't able to make contact with my taste buds, because of the thick quesadilla coating I had going on. It was as if the inside of my mouth had been sprayed with New Shit-Flavored Pam. I ate an entire hot fudge sundae without tasting it; I could only notice the temperature of my mouth decreasing. Then I handed them twenty of the dollars I'd earned at my my job, and left.

We went to Barnes and Noble afterwards, but everything is so expensive you pretty much have to make plans to buy something. You've got to budget for it, and check reviews and do your research. There's no impulse purchases of $35.00 hardcover books, at least not by me. And why don't they have fiction in their discount section anymore? All they have are big picture books about motorcycles and battleships and shit. Are there people who actually purchase such items? We wandered next door to the Eddie Bauer outlet next, to look at tables full of $75.00 sweaters that had been marked down to the crazy blowout price of $60.00 each!! Yeah, right. Like my spiritual leader Kid Rock, says, "I was born at night, but not last night, baby."

I guess Toney got a headache or something, because she said she wanted to go home after that. So we went home, and I decided to walk to the State Street Bar for a couple pints of Yuengling with the locals. But I'd forgotten that it was Friday (it felt like Saturday), and the place was crawling with people just off from work, chain-smoking and drinking as if they were engaged in a contest of some sort. I took the only seat at the bar, and ordered a lager. "Seventy-five cents," the bartender said after he'd placed the fizzing glass on the napkin in front of me. "Pardon?" I said. "It's happy hour," he said, "Yuenglings are seventy-five cents until six o'clock." Things got a lot better after that.

The world would be a much better place if every business offered reasonably priced draft beer. Little details like that make all the difference, I've learned.

— We haven't told him yet, but our dog's balls are coming off on November 6. We have a coupon. Do they actually cut them off, or just unplug them? I'm unclear, but I have a feeling somebody's not going to be happy with whatever route they take.

— I watched with sadness as my beloved Atlanta Braves were eliminated from yet another post-season Sunday night. And to add insult to injury they were beaten by one of those fake baseball teams, the Arizona Diamondbacks. Call me crazy, but I have a hard time respecting any team that wasn't in existence when I started following baseball, in the mid-'70s. I'm just now begrudgingly accepting the Mariners and Blue Jays, but I'm a long way from warming up to the Diamondbacks and the Devil Rays — or even those Florida Martins, or Merlins, or whatever they're called. And it makes me sick to see one of them going to The World Series, for God's sake. I'd say thirty or forty years need to pass before an expansion team should be allowed to make it to the World Series. Anything else is just… wrong. Also, was Fox using one of those Afghanistan Videophones to broadcast the game? What the hell was going on with that? Did they get a bunch of cameras from the old Soviet Union or something? I noticed the Yankee games are coming in crystal clear though. What's the deal? Hello, Art Bell?

See ya next time, boy and girls.

October 25, 2001

— I'm writing to you this morning (it's 5:40 in the AM) from our dining room table, using my work-issued laptop, because I'm unable to access the bunker. Toney's mother and her husband arrived last night, for a two-week visit, and they're piled-up in the room next to my office. I'm mildly resentful, sure, but the alternative is maybe kicking somebody's head in the dark, and accidentally getting everything cranked up two hours early. Being stubborn could very well get me an extra hundred minutes or so of amplified commentary on world events, and spoken-word op-ed pieces laced with the phrase "Jew bastards." So I'm writing to you this morning from our dining room table.

— They won't fly (especially after the Jews hijacked all those planes), and their hearts weren't into driving cross-country again, so Toney's folks decided to give Amtrak a try. It took them four days to get here. Four days! A flight would've taken about four hours, but whatever. They said that sometime during the middle of the night, around Denver, a 500 lb shoeless man was apparently forklifted onto the train, and he laid in the floor reading a book and saying, "Hi, how ya doing?" all the way to Harrisburg, PA. The guy was obviously too big to fit into a conventional people chair, so they just had him lying in the floor, between the seats. Toney's mother said every time she got up to use the bathroom or get a cup of coffee she had to walk past his "big fat sausage toes" sticking out into the aisle. They said he never got up (probably wasn't able to), he just laid there smiling and reading, a jiggling mound of flesh with a human head on top.

— Speaking of parents, I thought about my Dad yesterday when I was at Wendy's for lunch. I was accessorizing my meal at the condiment bar, when a thirteen or fourteen year old boy walked up and grabbed a straw. Such a thing would've been unthinkable when I was his age, because my Dad had some kind of hang-up about males using straws. Yes, you read that correctly. He called them "sissy sticks" and would make fun of you. So, to this day, I'm unable to use a straw to drink a soda; I'd feel like I was slow-dancing with a dude. What can I say? It's part of me now. He also had a problem with men using the word "wallet" for some reason. Billfold was the only acceptable term…wallet was fruity. So I say billfold, and never wallet. Hey, I know some of this isn't pretty, but we serious journalists are charged with reporting the raw facts.

— One day over the weekend I went into the basement to grab my first Yuengling of the day and when I opened the door to go down the steps I heard a loud roaring sound and was punched in the face by a chlorine smell. What in the honey-baked hell?! I raced down the steps to find water shooting out of some unknown white plastic tube hanging from the ceiling, and all over the wall at the rear of our house. And it looked like it had been at it for quite some time. Dammit! I found a little lever at the top of the tubing, and turned it until the water stopped, but a lot of shit was soaked. I wiped up the important stuff (like Toney's boom box), then did what every mature adult homeowner does: I called my Daddy.

I learned that the tubing in question led to the icemaker in our refrigerator, and he told me it would be a fairly easy thing to repair. Of course I was skeptical…an easy thing for him to repair, not me. But he gave me detailed instructions and it did sound pretty simple, so I decided to give it a shot. The next day.

A couple days later I felt I couldn't put it off any longer so I returned to the scene of the crime, determined to be a real man and engage in some hardcore home repair. Of course it wasn't as easy as good ol' Dad made it sound, and everything quickly went to hell. And I instantly became agitated and could barely contain the urge to hurl my adjustable wrench through the window. I had to call him back a couple more times for advice, and he began addressing me sarcastically as "Mr. Fix-It" (it's a wonder I'm not a serial killer). After about three of these calls it was painfully obvious that I was going to need to go to Home Depot for a "farrel" or "furrel" or some shit. I hate Home Depot, but what choice did I have?

It took me about five minutes to get into it with one of the hot-shot employees, because he thought he had all the answers. I left him standing in Aisle 31, red in the face, screaming, "It's not a coupling, it's a farrel!! It's not a coupling, it's a farrel!!!" Hey whatever, dude. I eventually found a wall of tiny drawers, and began pulling them out one by one. Finally I found what appeared to be the right item and made my way to the register with it, careful to let Mr. Hot Shot in the orange vest witness my act of defiance.

Yeah, it didn't work. I'm sure it has something to do with me, but I could never get it to stop leaking. I think I actually made it worse. So I just said screw it, and we filled up some ice trays. It's not the end of the world; people have made do with ice trays for decades. My Mom and Dad will be here for Christmas, and he can probably take two minutes out of one of his days, and repair it for me. The ridicule will most likely stop in a week or two, and everything will then be back to normal.

— The evening after I threw in the handyman towel, Toney told me about a conversation she'd had with my Dad when they were here a few weeks ago. Apparently they were discussing what a big dumbass I am, and Toney told him she wishes I'd picked up some of his talents for working on cars. He assured her that he'd tried to teach me some things when I was a kid, but that I'd always need to go in for a glass of water or something, and he'd find me an hour later lying on my bed listening to records.

Yep, it's nice to have a good solid support network.

See ya in a day or two.

October 29, 2001

— On Saturday we and Toney's folks went to a Chinese buffet for lunch. Naturally they hated it. They complained about the food, the prices, and the service (at a buffet!). They were also raising a ruckus about the "octopuses" in one of the entrees. "Can you imagine one of those tentacles flopping out of the corner of your mouth!?" they practically shouted in the crowded restaurant. Actually, I'm with them on that one. Just not so loudly.

— On Sunday we made another attempt at capturing some of that elusive Norman Rockwell magic by attending a Fall Festival. Basically it was just a bunch of food booths and the like, as well as games and stuff for kids. The howling wind had died down, and there was no snow, so it wasn't too bad. I was looking forward to checking out the much-ballyhooed "haunted locker room" at the middle school. I was excited to see what they'd done with it, but was ultimately disappointed. The possibilities were numerous. I was picturing Satan's Tampon Dispenser, and swooping flocks of vampire jock straps, but there was nothing of the sort. It was just a bunch of skeletons hanging on strings, and a few rubber rats peaking out of lockers. Lame, lame, lame. Next year I need to volunteer for that particular committee. The haunted locker room could stand a high-pressure Surf Report enema.

Sunday night Toney and I slipped away for beer and appetizers in the late afternoon. I talked her into trying the State Street Bar and Grill, home of the formerly seedy John K's Pub. She hated John K's but I assured her it's a lot more upscale these days. The dumpster out front is gone, for instance. She hesitantly agreed, but it didn't work out. They seated us in a room by ourselves, and handed us a pretentious menu which didn't contain any food that I recognized from the first 38 years of my life. There were no nachos or mozzarella sticks or anything like that. They had trout tacos, and mushroom towers, and crap that I simply wasn't able to comprehend. We just drank our beers and left. They used to sell hot dogs in that place! And club sandwiches!! So sad to see the fall of a once proud neighborhood tavern.

We went to a real drinkery, JJ Bridjes, and had nachos and Yuengling. We sat by the fireplace, and it was perfect. We don't do that often enough. When we were leaving we saw a man and woman having dinner, and the woman was reading a paperback book! They probably do that all the time.

We went home and eventually had dinner, then I got into a heated argument with my brother over the phone, and then it was time for bed and some rest before the start of another week in Rockwellian paradise.

Please keep in mind that these are only the highlights of my weekend. I live on the edge, boyee.

November 1, 2001

— Ninety-two days have now passed since we last purchased salt.

— I bought a cool 50-inch wide panoramic photo of my hometown (taken on September 23, 1924) in an eBay auction. It arrived in the mail yesterday, and you can clearly see laundry hanging on clotheslines, and outhouses in backyards, and dirt roads, and a thousand other tiny details. I can't really get my footing as to where the photo was taken, from what vantage point, but I plan to have it framed by Christmas and get my parents' input. My dad knows that town like the back of his hand and he can probably tell me the family history behind each house. The next obvious step is to take a similar picture from the same spot today. Is that too geeky?

— I had to turn the porch light off at nine o'clock last night, because of late-arriving trick or treaters. I think some teenagers get off on being menacing and making people feel ill at ease by continuing to ring doorbells well after the accepted cut-off time. But at least the ones here wear costumes. In California we would get people in regular street clothes banging on our door at ten, demanding candy, then driving off in a car parked at the end of the block. It goes against the grain to hand over mini Snickers bars to "kids" wearing cologne. One time a group of girls, well into their child-bearing years, came to our door, and a couple were smoking. Bored-looking teenage girls dressed in half-assed costumes and smoking cigarettes were on our front porch expecting me to hand them candy. Yes, it was a scene straight off the Saturday Evening Post. One didn't even have a bag with her. She just held out her hand, and then stuffed everything inside her bra. I'm not making this stuff up. We used to have two bowls of candy: the good stuff for the real kids, and the shitty cheap-ass crap for the brooding teenagers. It's not as bad here yet, but give 'em a couple of years to catch up. Things move slow in Scranton.

— I can't confirm this but I heard rumors that some do-gooders down the block were handing out toothbrushes and travel sized tubes of Crest last night. If ever there was a house just asking to be hit with a raw egg cluster-bomb, that's it. The audacity!

November 5, 2001

— All last week Toney's mother and step-father hashed out plans to drive to South Carolina to visit Toney's sister, and it involved the use of one of our vehicles. I wasn't thrilled about it, but it wasn't the end of the world either. After all, there was something in it for us - we'd get our house back for a few days. So, after a hundred or so changes to the plans (and after having to tell them that, no, they couldn't use my truck…and shaking my head at the sheer balls of the request) they finally left on Friday morning, in Toney's car.

I was looking forward to watching my new Pink Flamingos DVD Friday night, and having a few leisurely Yuenglings, perhaps even indulging in some husband/wife activities if the mood was right. But by noon they had called and told us they were on their way back. It was too windy to continue on. They had made it to Harrisburg, PA, and were turning around…because the wind was blowing.

I felt foolish for not even considering it as a possibility. I like to kid myself I've got them figured out, but I'm clearly out of my league here. I'm nothing more than a lightweight in this game. They're the '27 Yankees, and I'm B.J. Surhoff. They're John Lennon, I'm John Parr. They: Jack Benny. Me: David Arquette. Who am I fooling?

So, no Pink Flamingos, no husband/wife, a lot less Yuenglings than the situation called for…just the Fox News Channel at full concert volume and a lot of coughing and sighing. This is my life.

— Somehow, since the in-laws' arrival, the toilet seat in the downstairs bathroom has become completely liberated from its hinges. It just sits on top of the bowl now, balanced. You have to line up all the holes and be careful not to shift your weight while sitting there, lest you slide off and end up in the floor with your balls mashed underneath a wooden ring and your entire bodyweight. We've lived here almost two years, and the seat has remained attached to the toilet, but now it's a free agent. Coincidence? You asking me?

— Speaking of balls (how did this become today's theme?), our dog Andy will be howling goodbye to his set tomorrow. I can't tell you how guilty I feel about this. He trusts me. What good does this do, anyway? It's not as if he's out roaming the streets and mounting everything that casts a shadow. He's not Gary Condit. He comes from a good family, dammit. He lives in our house, and his balls haven't caused a single problem to date. But, oh no, society says they have to come off. I think Bob Barker started all this nonsense. He's got a lot of nerve having a last name like that and advocating such a practice. I think I read somewhere that he doesn't even really care about animals anyway, he's just trying to impress Betty White. I don't know if that's true, but I choose to believe it. My poor dog's balls are doomed to ruin so a horny old game show host can have a shot at bedding Betty White. Seems fair to me.

— Have I mentioned that Andy has a microchip under his skin? It's true. He came from the pound, and before they handed him over to us they injected a chip in his neck. I'm not real clear on what the deal is, but I think they can scan him like a can of Hormel Chili and pull up his mailing address and medical history. Hell, how do I know they won't install a listening device in his nutsack tomorrow? I'm going to be on high alert, and if I notice feedback coming from his crotch when he gets near the cordless phone base, I'm calling…somebody.

— On Friday I stopped at the beer store on my way home from work, and some asshole in the parking lot pissed me off. When I was walking away from my truck I activated the alarm, because my laptop was inside, and some redneck covered from head to toe in retina-searing NASCAR-wear said, "You've got an alarm, on that?" The hell?! It's a '98 Toyota, not the Sanford and Son truck, you pig-fucker. Is it so shocking that it came with an alarm system? Should I be embarrassed about this? And why the hell do you shit-kickers think you have a license to comment on anything vehicular, anyway? It hacked me off and that apparently came through in my expression, so the guy started making a half-hearted attempt at apologizing and backpedaling. His bodysuit rustled with the effort. I said nothing, but now I'm paranoid about using the (factory installed, dammit!) alarm on my pickup. It's like that episode of Seinfeld, when the guy calmly called Elaine "Big-head" and she spent the rest of the episode convinced her head was abnormally large: "I'm a walking candy apple!!" That's what the bastard's done to me.

— I went bowling with my father-in-law yesterday, and I'm simply horrible at it. I used to be at least decent, but now I'm like an arthritic monkey out there. I feel awkward, like there's a stick jammed up my ass, and I'm suddenly unable to bend at the waist. I bowled 123 the first game, then 91. 91! Stephen Hawking could do better than that. When we were almost done, I noticed a guy from work standing in the shadows watching. Why, Lord?

— The index finger on my right hand has been twitching all morning. This is how it all started with Michael J. Fox too. I'm going to spend the last thirty years of my life waving, I just know it. The shaky handwriting is on the wall.

More in a day or two, if I'm able to manipulate the keys...

November 7, 2001

— Yesterday was election day and the incumbent mayor in our town was re-elected with around 1400 votes, to his opponent's 7. I'm not joking. Hell, I could've done better than that, running on the salt ticket. Well, the fact that they close the bars on election day would undoubtedly work against me, but I bet I could do pretty well. Maybe I should launch a listening tour?

November 9, 2001

— We're taking the in-laws to Harrisburg on Sunday so they can get on Amtrack and start their four-day journey back to Reno. I've never traveled by train, but I'd sure like to do it someday. Heck, I'd like to do pretty much everything within reason. I like the idea of sitting in a club car and sipping beer late at night as sleepy American towns pass by outside. Every foot traveled is a million personal stories. I'd sit there and wonder what the people in all the houses were worrying about, and happy about, and looking forward to. Then I'd order another beer and do some more wondering. There are few things better in this world than new experiences, and beer. The in-laws are bitching about it, but I'm kinda jealous of what they're about to experience. Traveling cross-country by train? Sign me up.

I don't know much about Harrisburg but Toney tells me big black helicopters circle continuously over Three Mile Island these days, so I'm kinda looking forward to seeing that. If I can get some pics, I will. Of course there's a good chance I'll be shot dead by an overzealous National Guardsman hyped up on donuts and Maxwell House, but I'm happy to lay my life on the line to get a few cool pics for the website. I do it for you.

— Our dog Andy is recovering nicely from his Bob Barker surgery, thank you very much. He was moping around the first evening, moving close to the ground like a ferret and sleeping a lot, but now he seems to be back to normal. He's a real trooper, but it's going to be interesting to see what happens when we take him back to that evil house of nut extraction next week to get the stitches out. I have little doubt he'll go for some throats.

— The local Sam's Club has remodeled and one of the exciting new innovations they're bringing to Scranton is the Costco-style of distributing customer's developed photos in open self-serve bins. Most places require you to deal with a clerk behind a counter to get your pictures, but Costco just puts them out on the sales floor, alphabetized by last name. The old system only allows employees to sneak around and look at other people's photos, but the Costco system opens it up to the general public. When we were in California I never went there without flipping through a pack or two of some unknown family's snapshots. I guess it's a voyeurism thing, I'm not sure, but it's oddly exhilarating. It always made Toney nervous, like a group of people would walk up and catch me looking at a photo of their granny sitting in a recliner, but the chances of that happening are almost zero. Man, if this had been in style when I was younger I would've mixed up people's pictures, and inserted ones I brought from home, and all kinds of irritating things. I might've taken a picture of some random kid at my school, had fifty copies made, and put them in various envelopes. The possibilities are endless, but I'm too grown up to do something like that now. I think.

— Speaking of photos and hell-raising, it brings to mind something I did a few times as a teenager. My friend Mike and I would walk around at night with a camera, and knock on peoples' doors. When they'd answer we'd snap a picture and take off running. Then, a few days later, we'd mail them the photo with no explanation. Wonder how many sleepless nights that caused? Hell, we might've caused a couple of divorces. Good stuff.

— When we first got HBO in West Virginia (no, not last year, but that was a pretty good one!) everybody at our school pretty much watched everything and anything they broadcast. It was the coolest thing in the world to be able to watch uncut movies in your living room, with all the shits left in. I saw Car Wash like a hundred times for instance, that's how hard up we were for entertainment in those days. But I remember a movie from that era that absolutely scared the solids out of me, and I've been trying to find a copy of it for a few years now. It was called Stranger In The House, and it was a slasher flick about a maniac terrorizing a sorority house, and when they're finally able to trace one of his crazed phone calls ("Keep him on the line! I need more time, dammit!!"), they realize it's coming from

INSIDE THE HOUSE! It's sounds hokey now, but it had me squirting ice water when I was fifteen. Well, the reason I couldn't find any mention of the movie anywhere is because it apparently has a couple of different titles. I finally tracked down a VHS copy of it under the name Black Christmas(??), and I watched it earlier this week. It's not as scary as I remember, but it's still a lot of fun. It's from 1974 (with a pre-insane Margot Kidder) which predates the Halloween and Friday the 13th movies, but it's along the same lines. Another I remember fondly is Kenny and Company. Remember that one? Yeah, nobody does. But I swear it existed, and was really funny. I'm almost certain I didn't dream it.

— I was talking to my friend Steve a couple of nights ago, making plans for our upcoming trek to the Baseball Hall of Fame, and he casually mentioned that his wife Myra had had a bad day at work that day. My ears instantly perked up because Myra is a pathologist, which means she does autopsies and works with dead stuff. A bad day at work for her almost always makes my day more fun. Anyway, Steve said another pathologist, who is known for passing the buck (every office has its share of assholes I guess, regardless of the pay scale), passed off a rancid pair of legs for Myra to examine. Yes, a pair of legs — a nasty pair of freshly-amputated, pus and infection-filled legs. She said they were so rotten people were running from the room in disgust, and these are people who are used to rotten. I love it. Why am I picturing the legs sitting upright in the middle of a desk, with tube socks on? Yeah, it's funny but I couldn't do Myra's job even if I was smart enough. One whiff of some shit like that and I'd go down like Bobby Kennedy, I just know it. Holy shit.

November 13, 2001

— It's a difficult thing to fathom, I know, but I believe I may have had a little too much to drink on Saturday. In my defense though, I had some valid excuses: it was Toney's 36th birthday, for instance…and her mother was preparing to leave town.

She and her mother (AKA Sunshine) were out in the morning, doing whatever it is they do, and I stayed home to wrap Toney's gift. Actually I stayed home to get a short reprieve from the steadily building bitchiness and anger that traditionally comes when one of Sunshine's marathon visits nears its end. Oh, there's always bitchiness and anger, mind you, it just gets ratcheted way up when it's time for her to leave. I think she's resentful that we don't allow her to live in our house and run our lives year-round. This sounds like a joke, but it's really not.

I bought Toney a rather expensive robe she'd apparently been eyeing for a long time, on my lunch break on Friday. My hand was shaking as I signed the credit card receipt, and was wondering what was wrong with just putting on a big sweatshirt when it gets cold. And why wouldn't she ask for a more practical gift like, say, a Madness box set? I got through the process though, and when I asked the cashier if they offered gift wrapping, she practically laughed in my face. "You're dreaming, boy," were her exact words. Boy?! Is this like a real store?

Dammit. I'd have to wrap it myself, and I had no idea if we had any wrapping paper, or where to find it if we did. Everything you do leads directly to some other damn thing you've gotta do.

Saturday morning, after turning down the tempting invitation to join Toney and her mother on their shopping excursion, I said screw it and went to the dollar store for wrapping paper. They only had Pokemon paper, a bizarre Barney the Dinosaur variety with French writing(??), and some hideous dark psychedelic deal that didn't seem appropriate for any gift-giving occasion — except maybe a ceremony where a goat is sacrificed to Beezelbub. I opted for the sacrifice paper, and picked up some cool-ass yellow sunglasses that Toney later proclaimed "ridiculous."

The robe was in a square box, but it looked kinda round once I wrapped it. Apparently I didn't pull the paper tight enough. Who the hell knows? I'm pretty much useless when it comes to…you know, living and functioning as an adult. She seemed to like the gift, but didn't act very surprised. She'd probably been dropping hints for weeks. Good thing I picked up on them — the day her mother pulled me aside and told me what she wanted, and what size and color to buy. I'm nothing if not a keen observer.

So after she opened her gifts, and all that good stuff, Toney and I escaped by ourselves for a couple of hours. It was around two in the afternoon, and we made a beeline for a bar. We ordered a pitcher of Yuengling, and a giant pile of nachos called, appropriately enough, Nacho Piles. We sat there and made fun of her mother, and plotted our future. Most of our biggest life decisions have been made over pitchers of draft beer, which may explain a few things — but I'd rather not dwell on it. We're considering refinancing our house, and using the downturn in the economy to our advantage, so I felt slightly grownup talking about such things. Of course at the end of the day I know I can't even wrap a birthday present. Financial positioning? Real estate strategizing? Yeah, right.

It was a sad thing to behold, but the pitcher was eventually emptied and Toney wouldn't let me order another, so we dragged our asses home. We found Sunshine and Mumbles knockin' back the cocktails though, which was a pleasant surprise. They're a little easier to take when they're boozing it up, and it gets even easier when we join them. So I mixed us each a drink, then another. The edge on the day was starting to wear down. For an hour or so it seemed like everyone was having a good time, at the same time. It was an unheard of phenomenon.

After a couple of pleasant bourbon and Cokes we made our way to the restaurant for Toney's birthday dinner. We went to one of the roughly 7,000,000 family-run Italian joints around Scranton, and I promptly ordered another pitcher of Yuengling - you know, to get us through the menu perusal stage of the evening. Things were still going well at that point. We somehow got on the subject of office Christmas parties, and Toney's mother told a funny story about going to a big fancy dinner at somebody's house years ago, and when they flung open the doors to the formal dining room there were sanitary napkins beside every plate. The hostess screamed in horror and said, "Oh my god, my little girl asked if she could put out the napkins!!" Probably never happened, but it was funny anyway.

We were chugging right along, and I don't think any of us realized that the window of civility had already begun to close. There were no forks on the table when we arrived and that didn't sit well with Sunshine. It was obviously a personal attack. The restaurant management didn't like our looks, saw us parking our car, and raced to our table and removed all the forks - you know, just to screw with us. So that set the stage. Then the waitress was bitchy (she really was bitchy, it wasn't just a skewed perception this time), and that tipped the scales completely. Everything went south from there.

"Not a goddamn nickel!" she practically roared every time the waitress walked away from our table, "We're not leaving one red cent as a tip!" I was slinking down in my chair, and wishing she'd at least wait until our food arrived before berating the staff. I was convinced they were in the back-room pissing on my rigatoni. "Another pitcher, please!" I finally managed.

We somehow made it through the meal without a one on one confrontation, and without anyone being banished from the place for life, but it was touch and go there for a while. I witnessed her being banned from a diner in Reno once, and it wasn't pleasant. She was convinced the management had shut off the air conditioning on purpose when they saw her drive up — you know, just to mess with her. They finally told her to leave, and never to come back. It's like dining with Erin Brockovich.

I left a small tip on the table, careful not to let Sunshine catch me, and we left. I had another couple of Yuenglings at home and watched Pennsylvania Polka (the guy with the oxygen tank was on!), and some hokey old "rock n roll" variety show from the '60s called Hullabaloo on AMC. I was fading in and out by that point, but I seem to remember the Mamas and Papas singing "California Dreaming" on a stage amongst bathtubs with go-go dancers in them. I have no idea what bathtubs have to do with that song, but that's the way I remember it. Of course I had more alcohol in me than Peter Buck, so I could very well be mistaken. I also seem to remember seeing Jerry Lewis dressed as one of Paul Revere's Raiders and acting like some kind of idiot, and that couldn't have possibly been real, right?

— On Sunday morning I didn't feel too hot for some reason, but we had to take Sunshine and Mumbles to Harrisburg to catch an Amtrak train back to Reno, so I crawled out of bed fairly early. Things got off to a terrible start, nerves were on edge, and nobody was in any mood for putting up with anyone else's bullshit. Toney's mother immediately started complaining that she needed some donuts or something to settle her stomach. She said her "antibiotics" had upset her stomach.

She takes random pills that have been prescribed to her (and her friends!) through the years for various reasons, like aspirin. She calls them antibiotics, which may or may not be true, but they're definitely not being used for what they were prescribed for. And aren't antibiotics supposed to be taken over a week or so, and then stopped? She pops one whenever some "symptom" rears its head, like a cough drop. Years ago in Oregon, before I knew how crazy she was, she gave me some unknown pill that she swore would knock out my hay fever, and quick. I stupidly took it and my ears started buzzing and colors began swirling and I was knocked on my ass for about twenty-four hours. Lord knows what I ingested that day. I'm probably lucky to be alive.

But she wanted donuts, and I knew there was a Krispy Kreme in downtown Scranton. So we got off the highway, and promptly got lost. The bitching was incredible. The car became a rolling, seething buggy of hostility. When we finally found the damn place Toney's mother was screaming, "Just get some donuts!! I need something to settle my stomach! Antibiotics!...the anguish!...Oh, God!!" I asked Toney to come along and she snapped at me, "Just get a dozen glazed donuts!" And her mother hollered, "Glazed?! Is that all you're getting?? Gawd!!!" Everybody was talking at the same time; it was utter chaos. I said, "Holy shit, I feel like I'm in an episode of Mama's Family. My brain's about to explode!" I asked Toney to come with me, because I wouldn't be held responsible for getting the wrong mixture of donuts. And Toney's mother, apparently offended, said meekly, "Oh, we don't care what kind you get. Whatever you guys want." Ha!

The rest of the day was pretty uneventful. We went to Cracker Barrel for lunch, and Sunshine bitched about the food, but it was a relatively subdued performance. We walked around Harrisburg and it looks like a pretty cool place. It's old, like Scranton, but well-maintained - unlike Scranton. I could live there easily. There were little hipster bars and restaurants everywhere, and it seemed clean and safe. I was pleasantly surprised.

We took them to the train station, and that was really cool too. It was built in 1887, and looks as if it hasn't changed much in the last 114 years. I love that kind of thing, and walked around exploring for a while. The in-laws got themselves situated, and we eventually said our goodbyes.

As always, her absence was immediately felt. She's crazy and bombastic and reactionary and completely batshit, but she has a way of dominating a room. After she's gone calm returns, and it takes some getting used to. Last time I thought I was actually sad to see her go, which scared the living hell out of me, but in retrospect I think it was just the equivalent of that period when astronauts must undergo a radical readjustment after returning from space.

They called from Chicago Monday morning. Apparently people have been screwing with them the entire way.

November 16, 2001

— We've been here almost two years now, and I've decided to get my Pennsylvania driver's license. Something inside me says it's time. There's still about two weeks of life left in my California license, but there's no point in waiting until the last minute. To be quite honest, I'm not real conscientious when it comes to taking care of stuff like this. I got pulled over in Georgia once, after I'd lived there for years, handed the guy my (expired) North Carolina license, and he flew off the handle. The man completely lost his shit and threatened to impound my car and throw my ass in the "Jefferson Street Jail," wherever that is. For a few seconds I thought he was going to start pounding on me with his wooden stick; it was incredible. So this is nothing new. At least I'm able to hang onto some of the habits of my youth.

— A grocery store close to where I work, called Price Chopper, now has four self-serve checkout lanes. You just walk up and scan your items, and feed your money into a slot. It's bizarre. How do they know people aren't walking out of there with shit? How are they sure people aren't filling their carts with ham, and scanning a pack of Certs on their way out? This merits further investigation.

November 20, 2001

— We leave for West Virginia in the morning, and I'm braced for a long long day. Traveling on Thanksgiving is always a Montana-sized hassle, but it's gonna be even worse on the roads this year, because folks are afraid to fly. So it's gonna be ten or so hours of riding with other cars just inches away from us on three sides, and worrying about the dumbasses behind the wheels and what idiotic stunts they might pull. I hate going home for the holidays. I like being home for the holidays, I just hate the going part.

— At least we're not going to Reno. When we lived in California we always had to drive to Reno to break bread with Sunshine and Mumbles on Thanksgiving. I remember some horrifying trips up that long, boring slaughterhouse-lined highway. I remember traffic so bad cars were on the freeway in PARK, and people were out walking around and socializing. I remember seeing a Mexican gentleman pissing an awe-inspiring golden arch in front of hundreds of captive motorists, without even bothering to turn his back. The nozzle was clearly visible to all, and was equally awe-inspiring. I remember us driving with a giant futon tied to the back of our car, because we didn't need it anymore and Sunshine had graciously offered to "take it off our hands." Every time there was a gust of wind we almost became airborne. We were a hang-glider waiting to happen. I was convinced we were going to go off a cliff in the Sierra Nevadas, and they wouldn't find our headless bodies until the spring thaw. I was terrified that affordable apartment furniture was going to cause us to be eaten by grizzly bears. So, at least we're not going to Reno.

— We're going to have to take our dog Andy with us, and that should prove to be an interesting experiment. He's never ridden in a car for an extended period, so who knows what will happen? I'm envisioning projectile vomiting. Or perhaps he'll freak out and turn on us? Maybe he'll become terrified with claustrophobia and rip out our throats in a wild, savage frenzy? These are just a couple of possibilities that jump to mind.

— It's snowing like a bastard outside as I type this. Just like a bastard.

— I finally got my Pennsylvania driver's license on Friday, after almost two years of living here. Predictably it was a huge pain in the ass, and took way more time than it needed to. I sat there and watched the people behind the counter move as if they were under water, and couldn't help but think how politicians insisted on making airport security personnel government employees. Yeah, the skies are going to be much safer with these people in charge. But anyway, when I took my eye test the woman looked at me sideways and said, "Uh, you wanna try that again?" Shit, I thought, I'm gonna fail this thing. I pressed my face against the cologne-scented eye-piece and rattled off the letters again. She stared at me for a beat and finally said, "OK. Good enough, I guess. Have a seat." Whew. Perhaps I was too harsh in my earlier assessment; complacency and apathy clearly has its merits. I waited and waited and they finally called my name to take my picture. The Civil War veteran manning the camera asked me to verify that my name and address were spelled correctly on the form, and of course there were mistakes. Two of them. I considered telling him everything was cool, because I knew what was going to happen if I didn't, but I didn't want to carry around a license riddled with spelling errors for five years. So, I had to start all over. They stuck me at the bottom of the stack, and eventually got around to fixing their mistake. Stonewall Jackson took my photo, and there was more waiting. Finally, my license was ready. My fifth state! Pennsylvania falls.

I hope everyone has a safe and happy Thanksgiving. I'll be back on Monday, if Andy doesn't take out my neck on a Maryland interstate. I'll be with family for days on end, so there will undoubtedly be tales to tell. See ya soon.

November 26, 2001

Our Thanksgiving trip to West Virginia, Part One:

WEDNESDAY

— The refinance of our house had gone through and we spent the morning signing and initialing about two hundred sheets of paper in an office in Wilkes-Barre in front of a couple of besuited phonies smiling like Jack-O-Lanterns, so we didn't get on the road until after noon. We could've waited until we got back, but we were faced with the opportunity of not having to make a mortgage payment in December, so we hung around. No house payment, and no car payment in December. How cool is that? If we'd waited until today to sign, our month off would've become January and that just doesn't have the same feel. Maybe I won't have to snatch purses at the mall this year to buy us a Christmas turkey. And maybe Toney won't have to sell her hair to buy me a watch chain, or whatever.

— Our dog Andy had an expression of deep concern on his face as we forced him onto his blanket in the backseat of our car, amongst all our shit.

Oh, this didn't look good at all. What kind of foolish scheme had these people cooked up this time? Dear god, what are they going to put me through, and what is this shiny contraption they're trying to push me into? He refused to make eye contact with us for several hours.

— We saw the big black military helicopters circling Three Mile Island nuclear power plant near Harrisburg. Scary stuff. We saw two moving silently high in the sky, and another hovering closer to the ground. Shit. Each of those things are probably loaded with more fire-power than the entire country of Canada. And I thought my toll collector job was stressful!

— The roads were packed out with holiday travelers, and we were at a complete standstill a couple of times before we got out of Pennsylvania. But things got better the farther we traveled. Our bladders became swelled to the point of discomfort somewhere in Maryland, but the rest areas were simply out of the question. Too many hideous people in sweat suits, stretching and digging underwear out of their asses, and getting in my friggin' way. We eventually saw a sign for a state park, and got off the interstate to give it a try.

The signs directed us out an old country road, and we drove for a long time. I was worried we'd get so far from the highway we wouldn't be able to find our way back, but my concerns shifted suddenly when I heard Andy erupt in the backseat. He puked up a pile of maroon-colored goodness the size of a dinner plate onto the upholstery beside his blanket. When we looked back he was still smacking his lips. And then the funk hit us. Sweet Jesus!!

We rolled down the windows and picked up our pace on the bumpy road. I was on the verge of jumping on the puke-wagon myself, and Toney had her shirt pulled up over her nose. We finally found the park and it was completely empty, not another living creature in sight. It was an historical Civil War spot, a fort of some kind, possibly called Fort Frederick. Pretty cool — it sure beat the hell out of those shitty rest areas. We bailed out before the car had come to a complete stop.

I located the bathrooms, down a flight of dark stone steps behind an old log cabin, and found sweet relief there. Toney had all the doors of the car open when I got back, and Andy was running wild in an open field, terrorizing birds. A pile of maroon-stained paper towels was lying on the sidewalk beside the car, and Toney had a look of utter disgust on her face. I tossed the trash in a can, and went exploring while she made her way down the stone steps.

The dog and I walked inside the fort and looked around. Nobody was there and I wondered if we were even allowed in the park. It was kinda creepy. There were two big buildings inside and a lot of firewood and stuff. Andy was sniffing everything like a fiend and I walked up onto the porch of one of the buildings. And then I heard voices. They were coming from inside, and somebody was getting worked up about something. It was two or three men having a conversation, and things were getting heated. The hell? We high-tailed it out of there. I think I almost interrupted a Klan meeting, and nothing good could've come from that.

— The rest of the drive was uneventful. I talked at length about my plans for a clothing line called Famous Maker, which would have instant name recognition, but I got the feeling Toney wasn't really listening. We stopped at Cracker Barrel and loaded up on home cookin' and finally made it to my parents' house around ten o'clock. After we carried in all our stuff, and had a couple of the beers my Dad had so thoughtfully purchased for his son the drunk, we hit the sack. Another day in the life.

Tomorrow, the rest of the story…

November 28, 2001

Our Thanksgiving trip to West Virginia, Part Two:

THURSDAY

— Thanksgiving day. My mom and dad were cooking before I even hoisted my big ass off the bed. There was much clanking and smells of food coming from the kitchen as I had my first cup of coffee, and watched war updates in the den. I don't understand how a meal that will be enjoyed in the afternoon has to be started before the Appalachian rooster crows, but whatever. That's not my department. If I were in charge we'd go to the Old Country Buffet, then on to a pub for the traditional Bottomless Pitcher of Thanks. I tried not to analyze, and just enjoy. My mother is most likely going to undergo some frightening surgery in the next few weeks, and I've been appreciating her and my dad a lot more lately. I'm very lucky in the parent department, and that's no joke. I can't even imagine a time when they won't be around. And when those thoughts start creeping into my mind I force myself to think about baseball instead.

— My grandmother joined us for the day. My dad went and picked her up, from The Home. She's eighty-six (or thereabouts) and doesn't really know what's going on anymore. It's pretty sad. She had a big hand in raising me, but doesn't even know my name anymore. My mom worked when I was a kid, and my grandparents lived across the street. I had thousands of meals in their kitchen, and my grandmother counseled me constantly on how to be an upstanding young man. The fact that I turned out this way isn't her fault, she certainly gave it her best shot.

— I eventually drank enough coffee to get my blood moving again through my fat-boy arteries, and took a shower. Afterwards Toney and I flipped through the big stack of ads that came with the morning paper. Everybody was having "early bird" sales, designed to lure people into their stores during the middle of the night. You could pick up a 27-inch TV for like a buck, if you were crazy enough to go get it at five in the morning. Yeah, right. I wouldn't go to a Circuit City store at 5 AM if J.D. Salinger and Syd Barrett were there in sombreros, juggling torches.

— We had our Thanksgiving meal in the early afternoon, and it was quite a spread. I employed my usual rule of thumb and ate until I was on the cusp of a blackout. I've learned through experience that when the light-headedness kicks in it's time to stop. But it was damn good. Everything was good. As usual my mother tried to get me to "just try" the sweet potato casserole, but it makes me queasy just to look at it. I've been refusing that particular offer for thirty years now. I was relieved when they refused my offer to help clean up, and I waddled back to the couch.

— My friend Bill called and give me an update on the Commode Bowl, the traditional hometown football game between the Hillside Rams and the River Rats. In Dunbar you either live on the hill side of the railroad tracks, or the river side. On Thanksgiving day, every year since the late 40's, they have a football game between the two sections of town. They call it a football game, but it's a very loose term. Basically it's just a bunch of flabby drunks running around on the high school field in ridiculous get-ups. They also have a Commode Bowl parade (which used to feature an inbred man sitting on a giant toilet waving a plunger at cheering crowds!), and a "dance" the night before. Yes, it's quite the social event — almost a festival, in fact. Apparently the Rats kicked much Hillsider ass this year, which is as it should be, I guess. I missed it all, which kinda sucked. My parents live about fifteen miles from Dunbar now, so I didn't even make it to the parade.

— As we were recovering from our self-inflicted anguish my grandmother suddenly blurted out, "Where's the fence? I've gotta pee!" Yes, the fence. And no, I have no idea.

I know I'm stringing this thing out, but I'm going to have to finish this story tomorrow. There's more, but I'm late for work. Gotta go.

November 30, 2001

"I would've sent a shorter note, but I didn't have the time."

-Mark Twain, or some shit

Please allow me to apologize for the long-winded and drawn-out account of our Thanksgiving trip to West Virginia last week. My job is starting to cramp my style. I'm having trouble staying focused on the important stuff, but the fourth quarter will be over soon and I'm confident everything will return to normal shortly.

I'm going to sprint through the rest of this bitch, because I'm getting tired of thinking about it and I need to move on to newer things. I'm starting to bore myself, and that's not exactly a sterling indicator of quality. So, here goes…

Our Thanksgiving trip to West Virginia, The Final Chapter.

FRIDAY

— "Black Friday", to be more precise. Where the hell did that come from? I've never, ever heard that term used in conjunction with the day after Thanksgiving until this year, and now everyone's using it. What gives? Did somebody send out a fax? I don't even know what it means. Black Friday? Isn't it the traditional start of the holiday shopping season? Isn't it supposed to be a festive time? A bustling time? An exciting time? I'm confused.

— We were worried that our rambunctious puppy Andy wouldn't mix well with my parents' more established brother/sister doggie team, Pepper and Patches. I was imagining violent living room brawls, and lots of snapping and snarling and airborne dog slobber. But after a fairly short probation period (during which P & P sat around sulking and making sounds like fax machines) Andy was accepted into the fold…and he immediately returned the favor by taking on many of his host's habits and traditions. By the end of the second day he was joining them in their wild ape-shit barking jags, that can be triggered by a leaf falling off a tree, or a neighbor turning on a lamp in a bedroom down the block. If somebody has the audacity to actually walk past the house, all hell breaks loose. Those hounds lose their shit and commence to doing backflips off the couch and trying to walk up the walls, and creating a cacophony that you just wouldn't believe. It's incredibly annoying, and I think Andy actually managed to make matters worse by injecting some youthful enthusiasm. We pulled him aside and tried to explain that you're judged by the friends you choose, but I don't think we made much progress. He just looked at us.

— We went shopping in the afternoon, against my better judgment, and paid a heavy price. We went to several stores, including Sam's Club and Toys R Us, and they weren't too bad. I was pleasantly surprised. Then after a quick lunch at A&W (mmm…footlong slaw dogs and onion rings), we headed to another little shopping center down the way, and that's where everything went south. None of the stores are very old, in fact I don't even think the road they're on even existed when I lived there. This particular center includes Target, Lowe's, Circuit City, Pier 1, and a bunch of smaller places. Well, far be it for me to judge, but I think a slight engineering error was made in the planning of this place. You could get into the parking lot, but you couldn't get out. I've lived in Atlanta and Los Angeles and traveled all over the country, but I've never encountered anything like the mess we wandered into that day. It was absolute gridlock. No cops were on-hand either, just Lowe's employees trying to direct traffic. Sweet Maria! My blood pressure spiked, and I frantically looked around for an establishment with a liquor license. After everyone finally scratched their shopping itches, my parents joined the line of non-moving cars pointed toward the exit (we brought two vehicles, because they apparently thought we'd want to stay longer, and needed a getaway car) and we walked to a bar to try to wait out the traffic situation. After a few microbrews in stylish 22 oz pilsner glasses things didn't look so bleak. We eventually got out, but it was an unbelievable mess. A spectacular mess.

SATURDAY

— Toney and I wandered off by ourselves and checked out a few furniture stores. We really need some new furniture, but have roughly a dollar available to spend on it. Looking's free though, so we went looking. We visited a couple of places, and fantasized about how nice our house would look if we could furnish it with real furniture, and with pieces that actually match. Of course everywhere we went we had salesmen hanging around us, like ass-sniffing dogs. But then we walked into a place called Value City Furniture, and nobody would even make eye contact. We walked all around that store, up and down every aisle, and nobody said a word to us. When a salesman would walk by, he'd avert his eyes. It was very troubling. As irritating as it is to have salespeople constantly badger you in a store, it's even worse when they don't. What's wrong with us, we thought? We began to doubt ourselves, and examine our clothes and perform quick smell tests. I decided they had a policy not to bother people, but that theory was shattered again and again as they accosted every couple that passed through the doors. Shit. My self-esteem took quite a hit. I'm thinking about contacting Alan Dershowitz.

— I treated my wife to a very special lunch at a place in Dunbar, called Big T's Dairy Bar. When she married me she had to know she was getting herself into a fast lifestyle, and that's exactly what she got. I had a couple of West Virginia delicacies: hot bologna and white beans. Yum. Hot bologna is a sandwich with an inch-thick slice of bologna that's been cooked for a long time in barbecue sauce. I've never seen on it a menu outside of the Mountain State, but the rest of the world is missing out on a helluva treat. And white beans are great northerns, I think, and are just about the best things in the world. My grandmother made the best white beans ever, and I had them pretty much every day when I was a kid. I was in a state of nostalgic euphoria, with sauce smeared all over my mouth and hands, as Toney looked on with great concern.

— After lunch we went tooling around Dunbar, just checking out my old stomping grounds, then went for a pitcher of beer at a bar called Griff's. Toney asked me again about why there seems to be so much over-the-top state pride in West Virginia. Everybody seems to wear West Virginia shirts, and West Virginia hats, and have West Virginia stickers on their cars, and hang West Virginia flags from their houses. I told her I think it's because the state is constantly the butt of hillbilly jokes, and people feel defensive about it. I could tell she wasn't really buying the explanation though, which just goes to show you how much respect we West Virginians receive.

— We stopped at a convenience store and bought gum to help cover up the bouquet of barley and hops that undoubtedly trailed us. Lord only knew who would be at my parents' house when we got back, and alcohol is a sticky subject for some of the more uptight members of my family. But that store sells Teaberry gum, and friggin' Mallo Cups! Are they making that stuff again, or have they not rotated their stock since like, 1965? Holy shit!

— When we got home my mom played me a message on their answering machine from The Home, about my grandmother. A worker there was asking somebody to please come help them calm my 86 year old granny down, that she was "cussing and kicking" and wouldn't let the paramedics in the house to "work on Elsie." You could hear my grandmother ranting in the background. Man, oh man.

— That night we watched Monday's episode of Ed, which I had asked my mom to record for us. It was a great one, with Chris Elliott playing a freaky, cosmic lawyer. There was a classic scene where he took off his shirt in the middle of a meeting, with no explanation, and just continued on as if nothing had happened. I love that show. When it was over we kept watching in case there were scenes from next week's show, and Michael Dukakis's head suddenly popped up on the screen. The hell? Apparently she had recorded it on a tape containing the 1988 presidential debate! 1988. My folks are right on the cutting edge of popular culture.

SUNDAY

— Traffic was a bitch going home. We were at a complete stand-still before we even got to Charleston, which is just twenty or so miles away. I joked that we should've had somebody haul us back to Pennsylvania on a flatbed truck, so we could put the seats back and sleep the whole way. Not a bad idea, really. It finally broke free though, and there was a beautiful rainbow over the Monsanto Sarin gas plant (or whatever) as we left town. A tiny tear of emotion may have escaped the corner of my eye, or perhaps it was just all the chemicals in the air.

— We stopped in a town called Clendenin, on the other side of Charleston, to void our bladders and maybe pick up something to eat. There's an interstate sign claiming a Tudor's Biscuit World is off the exit, but we had to drive for miles to find it. I noticed my cell phone said NO SERVICE as we were driving deeper and deeper into uncharted territory. We finally found it in the downtown area, and it felt like we'd passed through a time warp. I'm not sure what era we were in, but it sure as hell wasn't 2001. We urinated to beat the band, and had some kick-ass biscuits at Tudor's. You can get pretty much any meat on a biscuit in that place. They had pepperoni biscuits, and I think pork chop and mutton biscuits too. We opted for the more traditional sausage, and they were good…damn good. Kick-ass biscuits.

And that's that. Sorry to be so long-winded. I'll get back to basics on Monday. Today's my birthday, so lift a glass to my continued decline, if you're so inclined. See ya soon.

December 3, 2001

— I've never much liked Sundays. I think they're highly overrated. Too slow-moving for my tastes. No mail, people lazing around on couches, businesses closed, the specter of another work week casting its insidious shadow over everything you do... So, by the time Sunday rolls around the weekend's pretty much spent in my mind. I think that's why they go by so quickly; there's only one good day in a weekend. It's almost impossible to work up a good Saturday feeling on Sunday. Saturdays are the perfect day. It's a day of possibilities and freedom. Spongebob, a little extra sleep, the knowledge that you've got two whole days in front of you that will allow you to be yourself. There's magic in a Saturday. I sure wish there were more of them.

— We spent Saturday afternoon doing Christmas shopping, and forked over an amount of money that, whenever I think about it, makes me twitch and grimace. Every year I'm convinced the celebration of the birth of the Savior will lead us directly into financial ruin — but we always seem to get through it somehow. This year, at least, it also feels like we're doing our patriotic duty with every purchase. Mock turtlenecks for democracy, if you will. Hey, whatever. Pass the beer nuts.

— As we were walking through the mall, a girl, maybe twenty years old, yelled in my direction, "Hey you, can you come over here for a second?" The hell? I looked behind me in a sort of Jack Tripper double-take, and realized she was talking to me. She was standing at the counter of one of those booths out in the middle of the mall, and I hesitantly walked over. She said I looked like I was about the same size as her boyfriend (?!?) and wondered if I would mind trying on some gold chains. Why me, Lord? Toney was lurking in the shadows laughing at my discomfort, but I stood there and allowed a fast-talking Puerto Rican woman to hang gaudy jewelry around my neck, feeling like the big dumbass I am. Finally, the payoff came as someone said I should be a male model, and there was uproarious laughter all around. Thank you. Thank you very much.

— I watched a little of the George Harrison death coverage over the weekend, and was mildly surprised that such a big deal was being made of it. I know he was a Beatle but, you know, he was Beatle George. I heard the BBC refer to him as "one of the greatest musicians of the 20th century." I don't know about that. I certainly don't want to be disrespectful, but I think people are getting a little carried away. I liked George Harrison, and am sad that he died so young, but this is a bit over the top.

— Dick Cavett appeared on one of the shows about Harrison, and that man is completely out of his tree. I can't hardly watch him; he makes me want to look away. His stories are like something you might hear at a Saturday night hoedown at the Alzheimer's House. He goes on with a bunch of crazy shit, then looks into the camera and cocks his eyebrow as if he's just scored big points with his devastating high-brow wit. The only problem is, nobody in the place knows what he's talking about. He waits for the avalanche of laughter, and there's nothing but crickets and the sound of people looking at their shoes. It's excruciating. I used to think Dick Cavett was funny, in a snobby Frasier-like way, but he's lost it. The man shouldn't be allowed out of the house.

— Toney told me a great story about the boyfriend of one of her Pennsylvania buddies. The guy is apparently a stock broker or something financial, and wears the suits and drives the cars and all that hot-shit stuff. He cuts quite the impressive figure, I guess, but he's nuts. He supposedly only eats with a plastic fork — a metal spoon, and a plastic fork. When he goes out to restaurants he takes his own if he thinks there won't be plastic utensils available. He also enjoys cola that's gone flat. She said he's very precise about the level of flatness, and keeps three two-liters going at all times in his apartment — each opened twenty-four hours apart. He rotates them out, day by day, in order to maintain that perfect level of flatness he so desires. How would you like to have this guy as your financial planner? Let me know if you're interested, and I can probably get his card.

December 7, 2001

— Scranton was mentioned in a recent article in the Washington Post by a columnist claiming to be in search of the "Armpit of America." My hometown du jour didn't take the top honor (that went to Battle Mountain, Nevada), but boy were people around here ticked off to even be in the running! "This is a great place to raise a family!…We have the best schools, and no crime!!…Our people are nicer than your people!!!…yakata yakata yakata. The whining was shrill and sustained — and the claim about all the nice people was nothing short of a bold-faced lie. I mean, really. But folks absolutely lost their minds over this goofy article, and the press reported the "news" of it as if it were on an equal plane of importance as America Strikes Back With Its Latest War On Terror So As To Achieve Enduring Freedom, or whatever it's called. The hubbub was really fun to watch, but I think a few people really need to check their ass-sticks at the door. I honestly don't understand how anyone could be so grim and humorless as to take something like this seriously; it's completely foreign to me. When I was a kid in West Virginia there was a Secretary of State who was really touchy (or perhaps just a showboating blow-hard?), and raised a big stink whenever the state was portrayed negatively in any national media. I remember him making a "march" on ABC headquarters in New York because a Love Boat episode featured Donny Osmond playing a barefooted, straw-chewing, overalls-wearing hillbilly from West Virginia. I can still see the news coverage of him and his small band of supporters outside the network with handmade signs on floppy Rite-Aid poster board, acting all awkward and stupid. Even at that young age I felt humiliated. It was the Love Boat, fer chrissakes! It had Donny Osmond on it. Nobody whose opinion mattered was going to mistake it for a documentary, something told me. Was I wrong? Am I wrong?

— We were talking about memorable holiday parties we've attended the other day, and two are worth noting here. Both were company-sponsored events, and both involved co-workers making fools of themselves after having "a few too many."

Years ago in Atlanta we were at a party in one of the conference rooms (they spared no expense), and we saw one of the secretaries hitting the sauce pretty hard. She was usually reserved and fairly conservative, a stereotypical housewife type, but we noticed her getting flirty and acting more and more out of character with each additional beverage consumed. We laughed it off and went about our business of draining corporate beers and making fun of everyone in attendance. It's the bond that's kept our relationship strong throughout the years. Anyway, a little while later somebody suddenly let out a big, "WHOOHOO!!!" and we whipped our heads around just in time to see this woman spin into the middle of the floor, as if launched from a cannon, with her hands above her head, thrusting and grinding her vulva like a Soul Train dancer. She had one of the managers in tow, and he was trying to keep up, but the music was clearly in her. She was making faces like she was suffering great pain, rubbing her hands all over herself, and pushing her reproductive organs to the fore. I almost swallowed my tongue. It was one of the most amazing things I've ever seen, and I've seen a lot. She left the company shortly thereafter.

The second party was at a mansion near Malibu, the CEO's house. Every year this guy opens up his residence to the great unwashed, and invites in all the employees at Home Office for a big-ass holiday bash. The place is simply unbelievable, a mansion by any definition. It sits on top of a hill, and is many, many square feet of tastefully furnished luxury. The spread of food is like something out of the movies, and there are always magicians wandering around, and fortune tellers telling fortunes. These are like no parties I've ever attended before or since, that's for damn sure. Some of my co-workers always refused to go, because of petty piss-ant class envy, but I was completely fascinated. Toney and I explored that house from top to bottom, and were amazed every time we turned another corner. I especially remember the giant bubbling fountain in the main foyer that would've been at home in the lobby of a Sheraton. And I remember a billiards room that was done in plum, everything was plum-colored including the felt on the table. Cool as hell. We snuck into the master bedroom once, and were amazed at their private bathroom. Not only was there a B. Dalton-sized magazine rack, but it also had two toilets facing each other! I had no idea rich folks shit together. Who knew? Interesting, I guess, but you can count me out! Their TV room was done up like a movie theater, complete with concession stand and popcorn machine and old theater seats. On one wall was a mural that showed the entire family waiting in line to buy tickets at an old-time movie house. It was probably painted by some famous artist they flew in from France or something. It was difficult to even take it all in.

But anyway, a person from Toney's department was there one year and spent several hours knocking back company-issued White Russians, and eating up as much food as she could hold. She was/is an excessively brash and cynical chick from Chicago, a little rough around the edges if you know what I mean. After her sixth or seventh drink she decided she wanted a cigarette, so she started stumbling from patio table to patio table asking for a light. This being southern California she didn't have much luck, and began to get frustrated. Finally she walked up to a table where three older women were sitting, and they told her they didn't have a light either, and preferred it if she wouldn't smoke around them. She instantly shot back, "Yeah, thanks for nothing, bitch!" And, as you can probably guess, she was talking to… the CEO's wife! She also left the company shortly afterwards, under mysterious circumstances.

I have a metric shitload more to write about, but the constraints of time are upon me. I'll be back Monday, if not sooner. Have a great weekend!

December 10, 2001

— It snowed here this weekend, our first real snow of the season. Even though we'll be thoroughly sick of it soon enough, the first snowfall is pretty darn exciting. I grabbed my camera and ran out on the deck to snap a photo for you folks, and almost busted my ass. It was slicker than cat shit on a marble floor out there, and my feet nearly betrayed me. I got your picture, but returned a little shaken. If I'd gone down I have little doubt the deck would've separated from the house and I would've ended up wallowing in the backyard with a redwood plank plunged into my back. I hope you people appreciate all the risks I take for you.

Saturday night, with the blanket of snow still fresh and undisturbed, Toney and I went out for a walk. She got a little annoyed because I had my pockets packed full of Yuenglings, but it was a really nice time. Nobody was out, and it was incredibly quiet (except for the occasional sound of a can opening) and beautiful. Like I say, we'll be cursing the stuff in a month or so, but right now it's welcome.

— Speaking of risk-taking, have you seen Geraldo reporting from the "front line"? Oh man, it's highly entertaining. His hair is all messed up, he acts nervous and jittery, and continuously looks over his shoulder and up in the air as he speaks. Of course it's all theatrics, but it's great fun. The other day he was giving a report and suddenly did a forward roll for no apparent reason. Afterwards he claimed that a sniper was firing at him. Hilarious! What a goofball. It wouldn't surprise me if we eventually learn he's really in the desert near Valencia, surrounded by Middle-Eastern extras from 20th Century Fox, and has dinner every night at Friday's in the mall.

— When we lived in California I became friends with Mark Maynard, co-editor of Crimewave USA zine, and we cooked up many a kooky scheme while sitting by his pool, smoking cigars and drinking beer. We both wanted to be big-time Hollywood comedy writers, but didn't have the patience for paying dues or learning the craft, or any of that bullshit. We figured we'd just bypass all that with cheap publicity stunts and blatant gimmickry.

We made huge sandwich boards on which we painted sayings like, "Will Create Gen-X Drama For Inordinate Amounts of Money" and "Repair Work: We Can Make Suddenly Susan Watchable" then marched up and down the sidewalk outside NBC, past hundreds of people waiting to get into The Tonight Show. That earned us nothing, except a brief conversation with NBC security.

We spent a lot of money by flying a professional filmmaker out to California to shoot a documentary of the two of us creating our sitcom, The Lords of Clairmont. We drove up to San Francisco, holed up in a semi-seedy hotel in North Beach, and hammered out the details of the show as the cameras rolled. The idea was to make a quirky little underground film that would be passed from person to person, and hopefully generate enough street buzz to cause some adventurous soul at one of the networks to actually give us a shot at producing the show. The UNEDITED master tapes are here in the bunker, up on a shelf. We never did anything with them, which is pretty damn sad — but typical.

We also read an article in Entertainment Weekly where Seinfeld honcho Peter Mehlman was quoted as saying something along the lines of, "If you're funny, come to Hollywood. We need you here. There's a real shortage of genuinely funny people in this town, and we could use you. Come by car, by plane, by train…just come." That's not a direct quote, but pretty close. So we started calling Mehlman's office and saying, "We're here!" Mark talked to Mehlman's assistant six or seven times, and their conversations were absolutely hysterical. Mark has a genuine talent for delivering the most off-the-wall shit in complete deadpan, and the other person doesn't know what the hell's going on. He told her we'd walked all the way from Kentucky because of the EW article, and were short of money so we really needed to get to work on a situation comedy or a film project soon. When she started to stammer in confusion he reminded her that Peter had invited us to California…indirectly, through a magazine article. It was classic stuff — also captured on film. But, predictably, she quickly grew tired of us and started making threats. So we stopped calling.

But we weren't quite finished. We made up a fake article from our "hometown paper", about two local boys who had been offered hot-shot Hollywood jobs by Seinfeld producer Peter Mehlman, and sent it by messenger to his office. The article was accompanied by a photo of Mark carrying me on his back down an old country road. He had told Mehlman's assistant that when one of us slept the other would carry him, so we could get to Hollywood faster and get down to work. That got no response, so we tried something else.

We decided to go around LA and take pictures of homeless people holding up signs we made from scraps of cardboard, which we planned to also send to Mehlman. The signs read: I BELIEVED PETER MEHLMAN. We took a few of 'em, but quickly lost interest in the "project."

— Here's part of an interview from the new issue of Spin Magazine:

Do you like Bill Murray?

Hell, yeah. Ghostbusters. Yeah, I watch a lot of shit, yo.

— I read that there's a sizable group of men around the country who get off by watching Deborah put lotion on her hands on Everybody Loves Raymond. I'd never noticed, but apparently she's often shown sitting in bed and applying lotion to her hands. People are sick.

— We put up our Christmas tree yesterday afternoon, strung the lights, decorated it, and watched helplessly as the bastard fell down in the middle of the living room floor. It was a nice day, with snow on the ground and the Elvis Christmas Album blasting. The Elvis Christmas Album is the absolute best Christmas album ever. We used to listen to it when I was a kid, and it still sounds great today. There are several Elvis Christmas Albums available, but the real-deal is the one with "Mama Liked The Roses" on it. That's the one that came out in the late 50's, and rocks the house. Toney's less enthusiastic about it, but I think she's coming around. She prefers the first edition of A Very Special Christmas. That's a good one too, especially the Run-DMC tune: "It's Christmas Eve in Hollis, Queens/Mama's in the kitchen cooking collard greens." Great stuff — except for Stevie Nicks doing "Silent Night," and that's one of the most godawful thing I've ever heard. It sounds like somebody's carving a ham with an electric knife. She sucks. Anyway, we were in great spirits. We'd just placed our favorite ornament, the glass pickle, on the tree, and had taken a breather to admire our handiwork, when out of nowhere everything started moving in slow motion, and it all came down with a loud crash at our feet. Quite a few things were broken, as you might expect, including a purple Santa ornament that Toney really liked. And the dog was slinking around like we were under attack. I didn't know a dog could still walk while that low to the ground. Yes, it pretty much cast a gloom over things for a while, but thank goodness for the Yuengling Brewing Company. Everything returned to normal fairly quickly.

Ho, ho, ho.

December 13, 2001

— I was listening to the stone-cold genius that is Phil Hendrie over the Internet the other night and he mentioned that he had wasted twenty years of his life, and it got me to thinking again about something I've thought about many times before. Even though I met a lot of great people during my twenties, and had loads of fun, I pretty much wasted that decade of my life. I worked bullshit jobs, dropped out of two colleges, drank too much, and generally underachieved as my school counselors predicted I would. I don't think I became an adult until I was about thirty, and even then the term was relative. I have friends who cruised through high school, right on into college, graduated and went on to normal grown-up lives, seemingly with little effort — while I worked in a record store for $225 a week and counted the days until Scruffy the Cat came back to town. Regrets? You bet your sweet pantied ass I have regrets. I was an immature dumbass for a super-sized chunk of my life. What's not to regret? ...Do Camaros come in silver?

— Toney went for a tour of a health club with one of her Pennsylvania buddies the other day, and it reminded me of my brief membership in such a club back in the Atlanta days. It was actually around the time I met

Toney, and I think I only went along with it to impress her (see above). We joined up together, even though my heart wasn't in it, and "worked out" after work a few days each week. I told myself to just give it a chance and I might end up liking it, but it never happened. For one thing, there were a lot of sweaty people there. When you walked through the doors you could smell people, and I'm just not down with that. It wasn't really sweat that you could smell, but a swirling cocktail of various commercial products designed to stop sweat from stinking. Disgusting. The machines were sweaty, the people were sweaty, the lines of sweaty people waiting to use the sweaty machines were long, and I had to, you know, work up a sweat while I was there. Not exactly my idea of a good time. I also felt like a fool sitting on those ridiculous contraptions in the middle of a floor, rowing and pumping and flexing. Who the hell did I think I was? I felt like a fraud the entire time, and prayed none of my friends in West Virginia would ever hear about it. And don't even get me started on the locker room! I've never felt so uncomfortable in my entire life — it was like Cocks R Us! The first time I walked in there I just couldn't believe it. Dicks as far as the eye could see, and everyone apparently just perfectly OK with it all. Fa-la-la, I'm so cool and professional I don't even notice your hyper-extended balls there. I remember groups of men standing around, just shooting the shit about their stock options or whatever, with their junk on full display. And I remember a bunch of guys huddled around a TV cheering something on Monday Night Football…with their penises bouncing up and down right along with them. And I remember a black dude talking on a payphone to his girlfriend or wife about picking up some steaks on his way home, as his myth-affirming unit swayed majestically to and fro. I could live to be 200 and never achieve that level of maturity. Holy shit in a handbasket.

December 17, 2001

— Remember how I bragged about how good our dog Andy is? Remember how I said he was remarkably well-behaved for a puppy, and caused us few problems? Well, I take it all back. The little shithead chewed up a leg on one our dining room chairs last week. A leg of a chair! Not a shoe or a glove or something, but a piece of furniture! I get pissed just thinking about it. He's lucky I didn't boot his ass through the front window.

Apparently not one to rest on past achievements, he also had a few additional tricks up his fur sleeve last week. Toney bought a postcard off eBay of an old, defunct casino in Reno called The Mapes, that her grandfather managed for a while, and planned to have it framed for her mother for Christmas. Well, that postcard survived for fifty years, but only about a half-hour once it made it to our house. Andy somehow managed to get it off the dining room table, just minutes after the envelope was opened, and chewed it up. We'll probably find bits of Toney's grandfather's casino sticking out of a pile in our front yard, a touching tribute.

He also got up on my chair one night, while I was in the kitchen, and finished off my dinner. Meat loaf, scalloped potatoes, and peas. What kind of dog eats scalloped potatoes? I was out of the room for the length of time it takes to pour a glass of water, and my plate looked like it had just came out of the dishwasher when I got back. All I could do was stand there. It's like a situation comedy at our house.

He's treading on thin ice. I'm not putting up with much more of his bullshit, and that's no joke. Everybody says, "Well, that's just the pup in him," but I'm not real interested in excuses. This ain't Oprah. I'm thinking about taking him for a little drive, back to the Humane Society from where he came, and show him the big black smokestacks sticking out of the roof. Maybe that'll do the trick. If he realizes he could end up as a thin layer of Border Collie ash on an awning across town he might get his shit together.

— I've heard plenty of canine horror stories through the years, and always huffed arrogantly that I wouldn't stand for such shenanigans — and yet here I am. My friend Steve's dog ate an entire section of drywall in their house, while they were at work one day, and they just laughed it off as part of the deal of owning a dog. Talk about having the patience of saints! And my aunt's cocker spaniel once launched into a wild frenzy and ate a ten pound bag of raw potatoes (again with the potatoes!) and a couple of apple pies, which he eventually blew out both ends like a shit and puke cannon in the middle of their family room. And my parents' old dog used to shoot spontaneous high-pressure oily-black jets of diarrhea from one end of the room to the other, and down hallways, and across fences — because of a digestive problem brought on by an all-hotdog diet, or some shit. Maybe a couple of three-legged chairs ain't so bad, huh?

— Like an idiot, I spilled a tray of food at Wendy's Saturday afternoon. I'm not sure why, but I tried to pick it up with one hand and misjudged the weight of the drinks. Everything dumped straight into the floor, and Coke splashed high up some stranger's pants leg. I felt like a fool, and apologized like mad as I made a frantic attempt to clean up the mess. Everybody was nice about it though, and told me not to worry, but I think they were talking a little slower and a little louder to make sure I could understand them. Shit. I've always had low tolerance for dumbasses who stumble around restaurants and spike their meals and drinks like they just scored a touchdown, and here I was doing the spiking. "JUST — HAVE — A — SEAT — SIR. WE'LL — CLEAN — THIS — UP. NO — PROBLEM. IT'S — JUST — GREAT — THAT — YOU'RE — ABLE — TO — GET — OUT."

December 26, 2001

Christmas, and my visiting parents, pretty much kept me away from the Internet for the past four or five days. It wasn't easy, but I soldiered through. I've been wearing a Yahoo! patch, so I suppose that helped. I hope everyone is having a happy and safe holiday season, regardless of the holidays you're celebrating. I'm typing this at the dining room table as the rest of the house sleeps, so I'm going to have to keep it brief. But here's a couple of things I've had on my mind...

— Toney and my parents pitched in and bought me a new stereo a few weeks ago, for my birthday. My old one just decided to throw in the towel and stop playing CDs three or four months back. I'd been forced to play shit through my computer, and that just doesn't cut it - there's not a lot of oomph in a speaker the size of a flip-flop. I barely even bothered. But now I'm back in the saddle, and I've been in a minor frenzy getting reacquainted with all my old faves. Robyn Hitchcock sounds especially tasty through my new phat-ass speakers, as do The Buzzcocks and The Kinks. I even went out and bought a copy of The Strokes "Is This It" a few days ago, in a lame attempt at staying current. Hell, at least I still try. It would be really easy at this point to just throw on Steely Dan, have a cup of hazelnut, and say screw it - but for now I refuse to die.

— During my recent CD frenzy, I popped in a disc of the so-called best moments from an Atlanta morning radio host I used to be addicted to. He calls himself Christopher Rude and I think he still racks up big ratings there, justifiably. The fact that I actually plunked down money for this recording is testament to...something. Anyway, back in the day I listened to his show every morning and I thought he was hysterical. I even remember Toney saying to me, "You've been ruined by Beavis and Butthead, The Jerky Boys, and Christopher Rude!" How's that for an endorsement? Well, the stuff on this CD sounds pretty dated today, but a good part of it's still funny. "Who Cut the Cheese?" still holds up, as does "As Turds Go By," but all the anti-Dave Justice material is pretty embarrassing (he had a long-running feud with the ex-Braves outfielder, and constantly played a clip of him saying, "I've got nothing to say to 96 Rock...y'all dogged me, man!"), and the Jeffrey Dahmer stuff is pretty tired. It was great radio in its day though, regardless of what Toney might tell you. I remember Rude telling a story that went on for five solid minutes, about going out to a martini bar with some people at the radio station. At the end of the night he dropped off the traffic-copter guy and he didn't seem to be doing too well in his progress to the front door, so he drove around the block to check on him. When he got back there was a puddle of puke in the street "from curb to curb" and his car fish-tailed when he drove through it. That killed me. I'm a sucker for people who can milk comedy out of everyday life. I also remember a game they used to play called Mind Melt. People would call up and be asked to name four examples of something in less than thirty seconds, for a Busch Lite party-pack or some such valuable prize. One of the questions was, "Name four famous places that don't really exist," and the hick on the line said, "…uhhh, Bumfuck?" I nearly flipped my car laughing. I know it sounds low-brow and dumbass, but it really wasn't. Christopher Rude made fun of the dumbasses, and they usually didn't even know it. When the station was bought-out by a giant corporation, they fired Rude and replaced him with a couple of syndicated shit-kickers from Charlotte. The uproar was so loud and sustained they actually hired him back — and it was no publicity stunt. How often does that happen?

I know this is a weak and strange update, but I'm gonna have to cut it short. We had a pleasant Christmas here at The Compound, if unremarkable. My parents are pretty sane, and don't provide an abundance of tales. It's the polar opposite of a visit from Sunshine and Mumbles. I'll try to crank out a proper entry for tomorrow, so stay tuned.

Bye, for now. I've gotta make coffee; I hear some stirring.

December 27, 2001

— There's been further fallout from the Armpit of America article I wrote about a few weeks ago. If you'll remember, the citizens of my latest hometown of Scranton were worked into a lather because their city was mentioned in the piece as a finalist for the unwanted title. Well, as late as yesterday angry letters to the editor were still appearing in the papers here. People just can't let it go. And now I read that a newspaper editor in the "winning" town has been fired for agreeing with the writer of the article! Man, I wish I could stir up this much shit with something I wrote. Just once I'd like to have old ladies praying for the salvation of my black black soul, like the ones who send letters to The Scranton Times. It would be a dream come true.

— I worry about myself sometimes. Every once in a while I get a mild urge to be mean to complete strangers. Oh nothing sinister, just the sporadic desire to trip somebody, or to body-check a son of a bitch into a random grocery store dairy case. And usually nothing even provokes these feelings, they just occur out of thin air. The other day in Wendy's a guy walked past my table after getting a refill of his drink, and I wanted to stand up and slap it out of his hand — for no reason. Then I started fantasizing about walking all around the restaurant, just smacking shit out of people's hands: a tray of food, a hamburger as it's being lifted to a mouth, Happy Meal toys. What the hell's wrong with me? Someday I fear I won't be able to suppress these urges, and I'll get my fat ass kicked and/or arrested. Am I nuts?

— Our dog Andy is going to start obedience classes next week. Toney is going to take him, and it lasts for eight long weeks. It was either that, or a one-way car trip to Philadelphia's Koreatown. He better do his homework too, goddammit.

— Sometimes I listen to an Internet radio station at work called Altern80's. They play lots of new wave stuff, as well as The Replacements and The Pixies and X, and the like. It's pretty cool but they have a little promo that comes on from time to time that says, in a deep mechanized voice: "You're living in the past." Gee, thanks. That's very flattering. Why not just throw in, "You're unattractive to the opposite sex," and "You have an unusually abbreviated sex organ"? That'll keep us coming back!

December 31, 2001

— New Year's Eve. Call me a freak, but I'm a little worried about Times Square tonight. I'm worried some second-string lunatic will set off an explosive of some sort, possibly even one of those Russian nuclear suitcases that are floating around out there. I probably shouldn't joke about this, but if they do have nuclear winter at Times Square tonight, does anyone doubt that Dick Clark will be the only thing to survive? Yeah, suddenly I'm the

Buddy Hackett of tastelessness…

— My parents gave me and Toney a new dishwasher for Christmas. It's cool, and it's appreciated, but it's not nearly as exciting as the days when I used to get a mound of toys. I remember coming down the steps on Christmas morning, literally shaking with excitement, and laying my eyes on all the cool stuff that Santa had brought. It was the moment the previous twelve months had been leading up to. Now I get a dishwasher, to replace the old dishwasher, installed days before Christmas. Santa hasn't brought me shit for years. I don't want to seem like an ingrate, because I'm not, I guess I'm just bitching some more about getting old. Couldn't somebody just throw me a bone and slide me an Ants In The Pants game or something? That's all it would take to make me happy. Five bucks, tops. A few evenings of flicking plastic ants into a large pair of free-standing blue jeans with suspenders is all I want. Is that too much to ask?

— Speaking of our old dishwasher, it was high time that it was put out of its misery. The thing was loud and didn't really work. It sounded like a blender full of spoons when it was running, and big chunks of macaroni and cheese would be practically welded to the silverware when it was done. I don't even know where the mac and cheese came from, it certainly wasn't there when we loaded it. I think we were picking up food residue from the previous owners — or perhaps the next-door neighbors! Anyway, it's pretty cool to have a quiet and efficient appliance to clean up our disgusting messes. This bitch puts out plates so clean you could practically eat off them!

— Yesterday we went to Target to get a refund on the coffee maker we bought a few weeks ago, that takes ludicrous little cone filters and turns itself off and on at random times. I was afraid the stupid thing would burn our house down, so we packed it up and took it back. As we were walking across the parking lot, the wind was blowing so hard I felt like I might actually become airborne. The shit was whipping, and I went up on my tip-toes a couple of times. Thankfully I'm anchored down by a thick flesh parka, or who knows what might've happened? When we finally made it to the front door I said, "Damn, I almost lost my hairpiece!" Obviously it was a joke, but a guy in front of us turned around and looked me straight in the eyes. He was pissed, and apparently didn't take too kindly to wig comedy. Wonder why?

— As I was flipping through the channels this weekend I stopped on something that showed kids running through the streets with one of those big round yellow flashing lights that you see at construction sites on the interstate. You know, they're always attached to those metal black and white workhorse things? I have no idea what the show was about but it made me remember how my friends and I used to steal street signs when we were teenagers. We'd usually take the ones that made some sort of rock reference, like Hendrix Ave. or E Street. Actually it was the thrill of stealing the things that I liked. I don't even remember what we did with them after we stole them — probably hurled them in the river or something. Anyway, my friend Mike wasn't satisfied with simple street signs, they were just a gateway drug and his addiction quickly escalated to the point where he took one of those flashing lights. I remember it had a heavy-ass battery attached to it, and he somehow smuggled it into his bedroom without his parents noticing. And the thing was bright! I remember being outside and seeing the windows of his room illuminated brilliant yellow, then dark, then brilliant yellow… It was hilarious. Mike was frantic after he got it into the house. It was inevitable that he was going to be caught, because it was pretty damn hard to conceal something that emits a retina-searing blast of light every few seconds. Where do you hide such an item? He put it under the covers of his bed and it still lit up the entire back-end of the house. He put it in the closet and you could see light on all four sides of the door. I was convulsing with laughter. Being the good friend that I was, I eventually said, "See ya!" and left. He got caught later that night, but his folks didn't make too big of a deal out of it. I think they just made him take it back to where he found it. My parents would've cornered me for hours in my room, repeatedly asking, "Why? Why'd you do it?" Shit, I would've preferred a good beating to that brand of punishment, but that's a discussion for another day…

That'll do it for today. I hope everyone has a great New Year's Eve, and New Year's Day. Hopefully it'll all go off without a hitch. I always imagine the worst in every situation, so it'll probably be OK. But be safe, my friends. Barring the instantaneous eradication of our skin and bones, I'll be back in a couple of days. See ya soon. I hope.

THE ADVENTURE CONTINUES!

I hope you enjoyed this collection of posts from the first ridiculous year of The West Virginia Surf Report. Stay up to date on the availability of additional volumes by visiting this handy page:

www.SurfReportArchives.com

If you had fun reading this book, I'd very much appreciate a review at the website of purchase. However, if you didn't like it all that much... why waste time writing reviews? I mean, you're a very busy person, right? Who has time for such nonsense?

Comments, complaints, and letters of outrage can be sent to my main email address:

jeff@thewvsr.com

And I thank you, sincerely, for reading. There's much more to come!

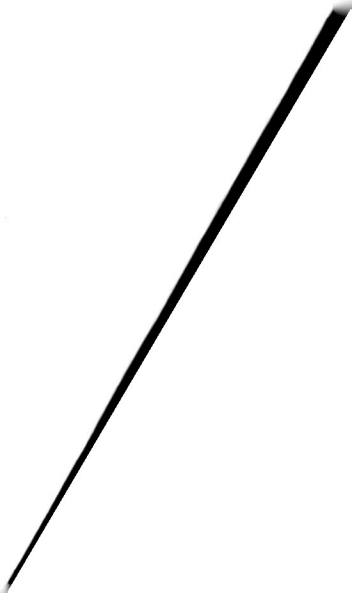

www.ingramcontent.com/pod-product-compliance
Lightning Source LLC
Chambersburg PA
CBHW061821040426
42447CB00012B/2762